BIG
ALPHABET BOX
HANDWRITING
PRACTICE
WORKBOOK

LETTER TRACING TO PRACTICE
CORRECT LETTER FORMATION

This book belongs to:

_____

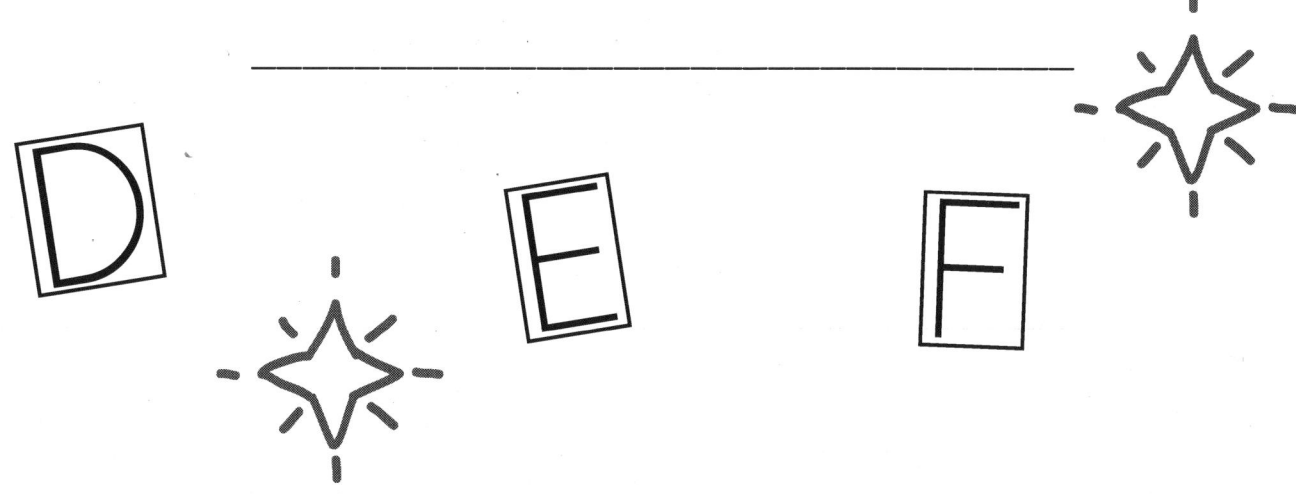

Trace the dotted lines from left to right.

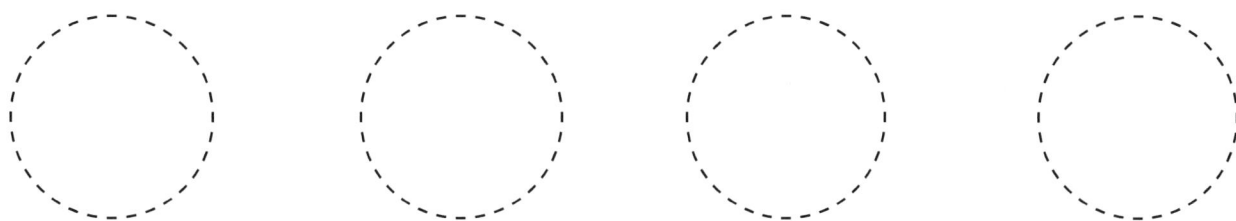

Trace the dotted lines from left to right.

A is for alligator. Color the alligator.

alligator

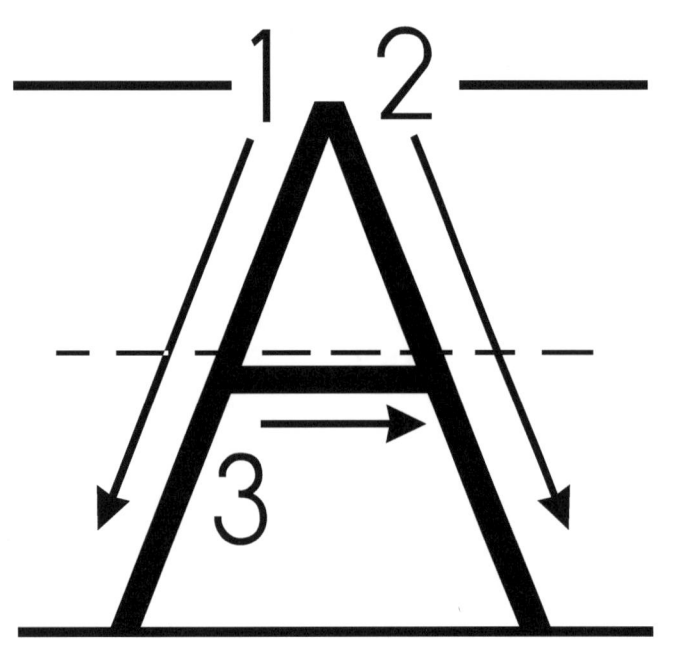

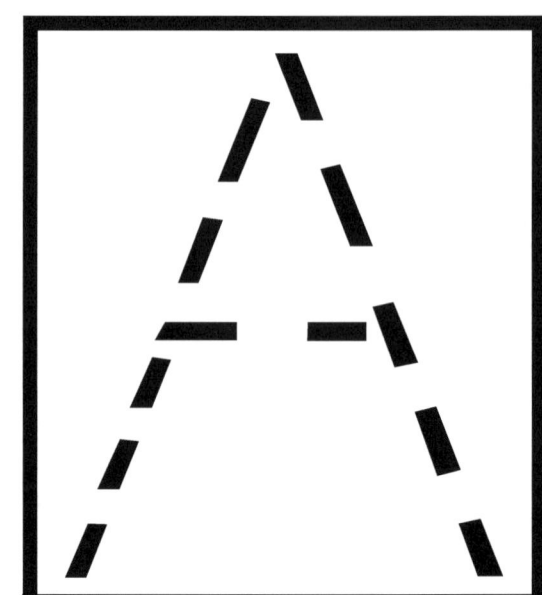

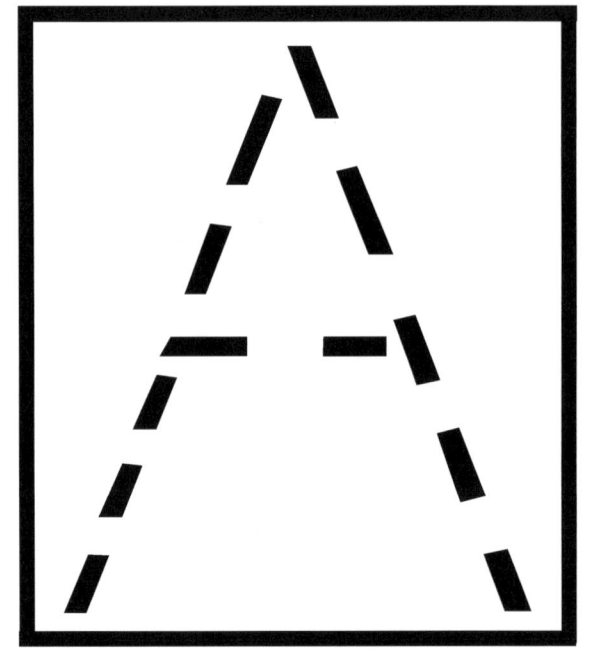

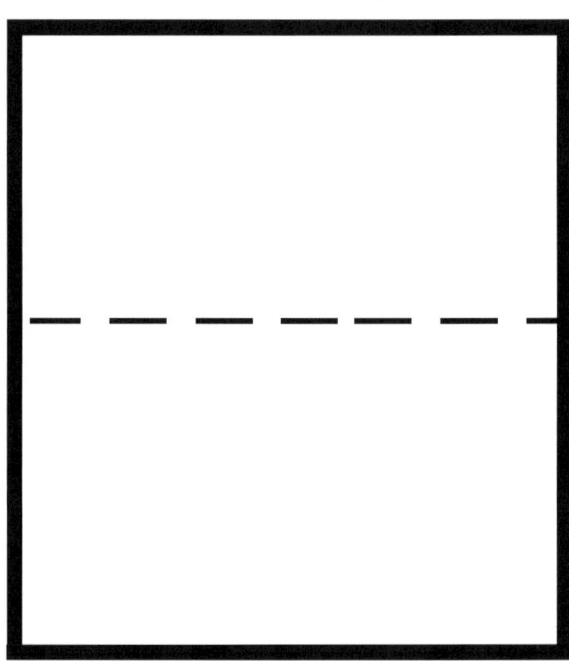

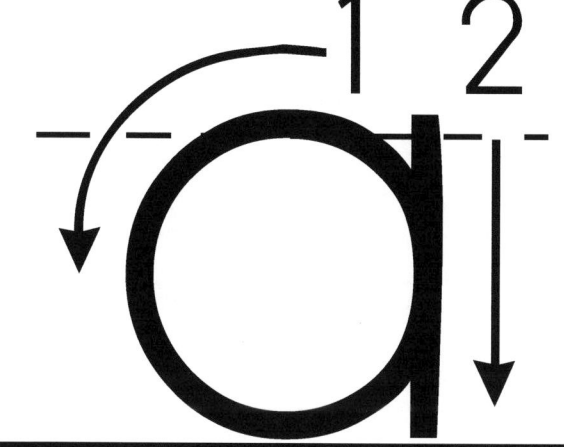

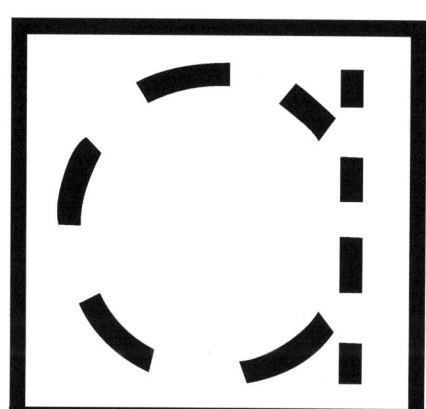

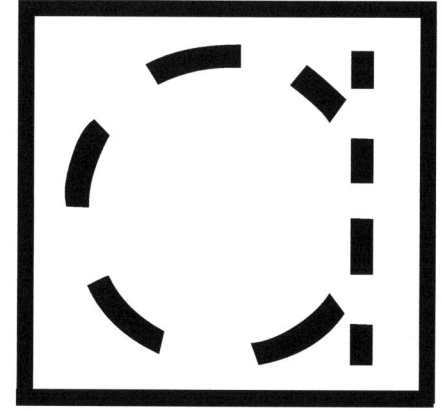

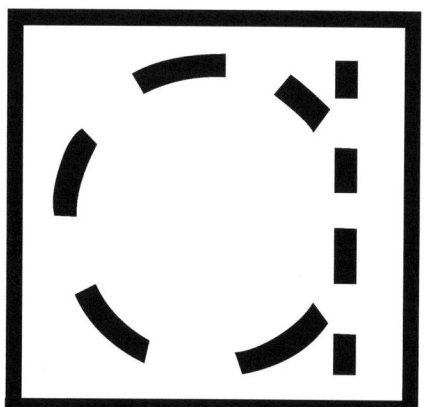

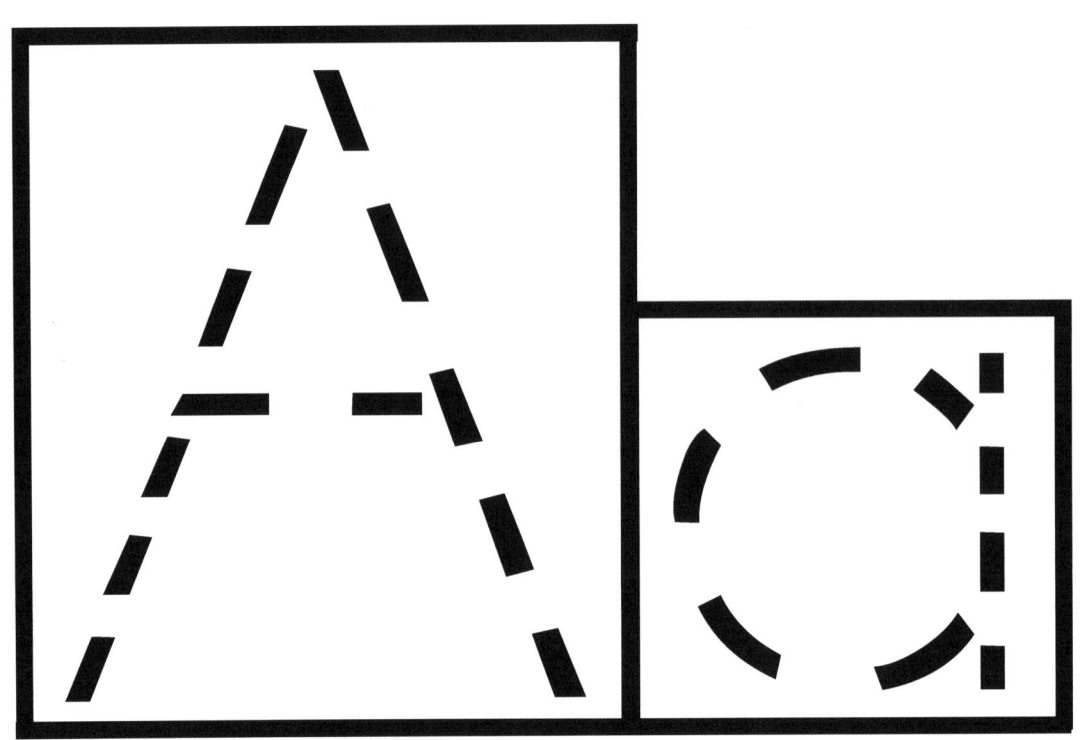

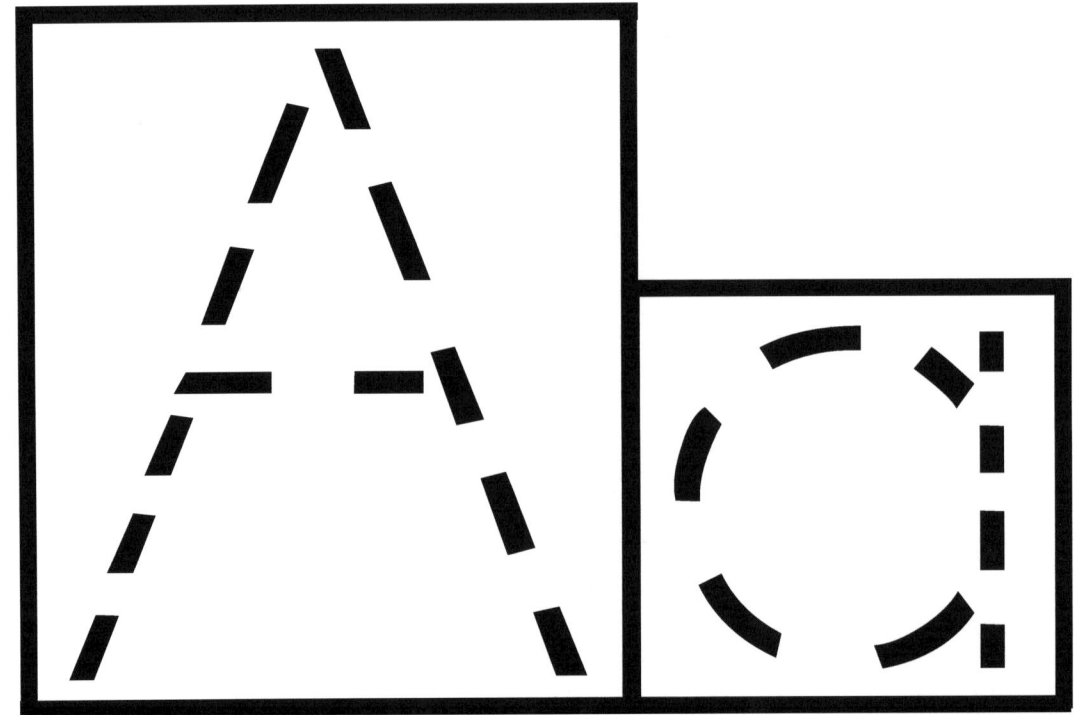

B is for butterfly. Color the butterfly.

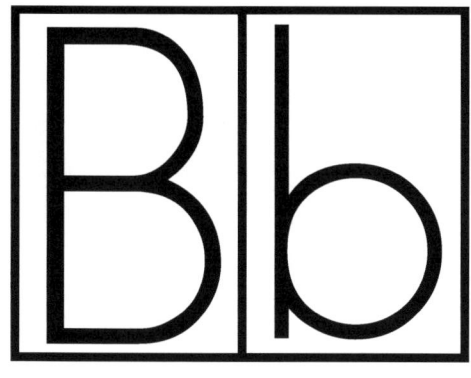

butterfly

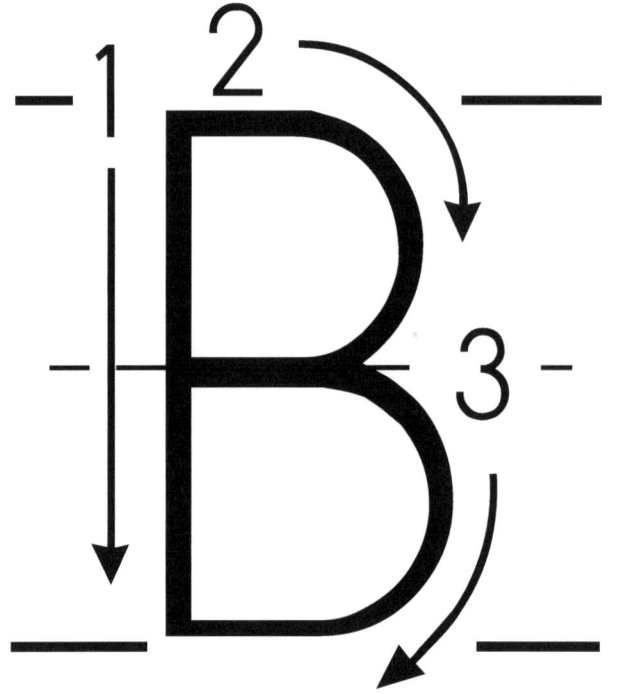

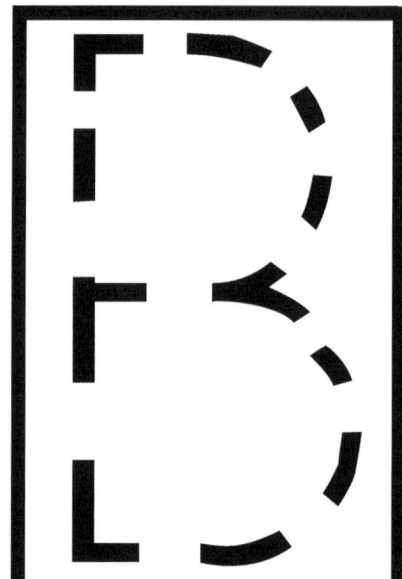

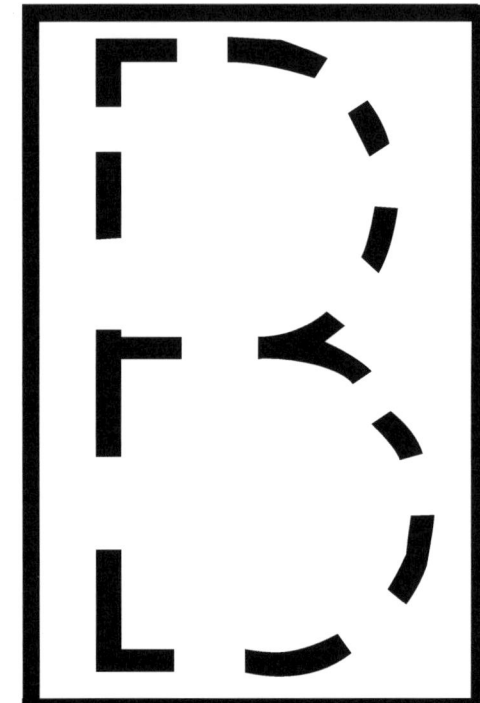

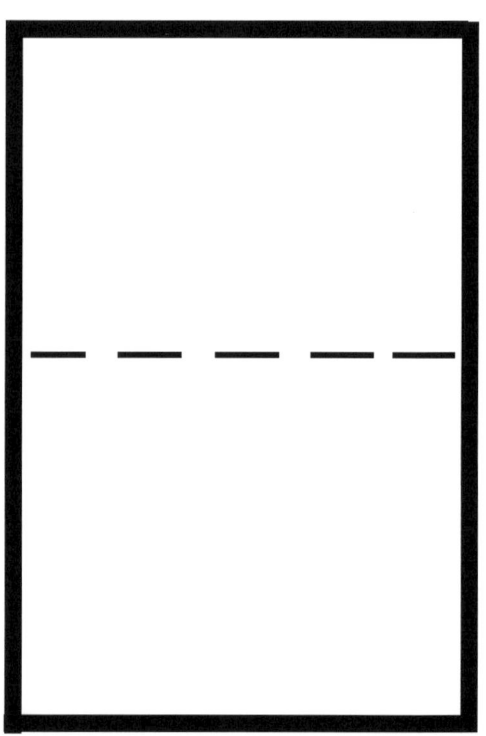

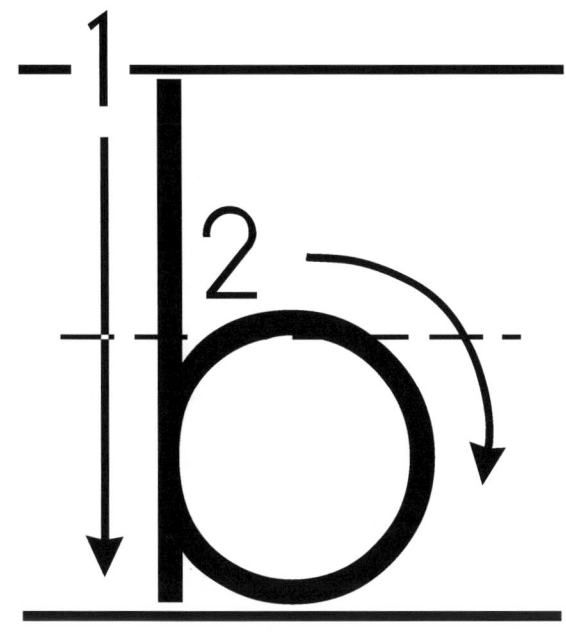

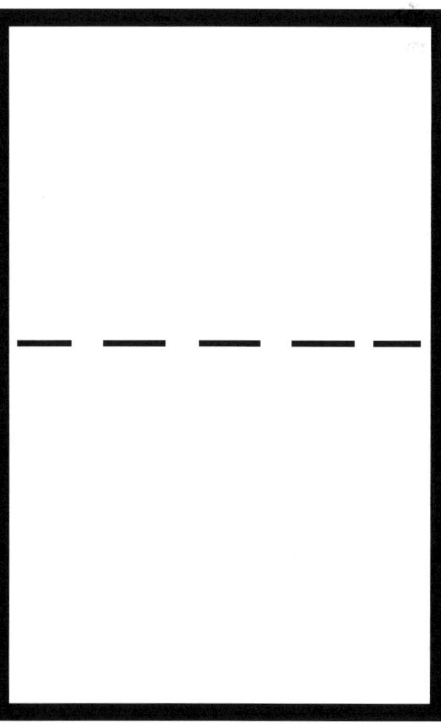

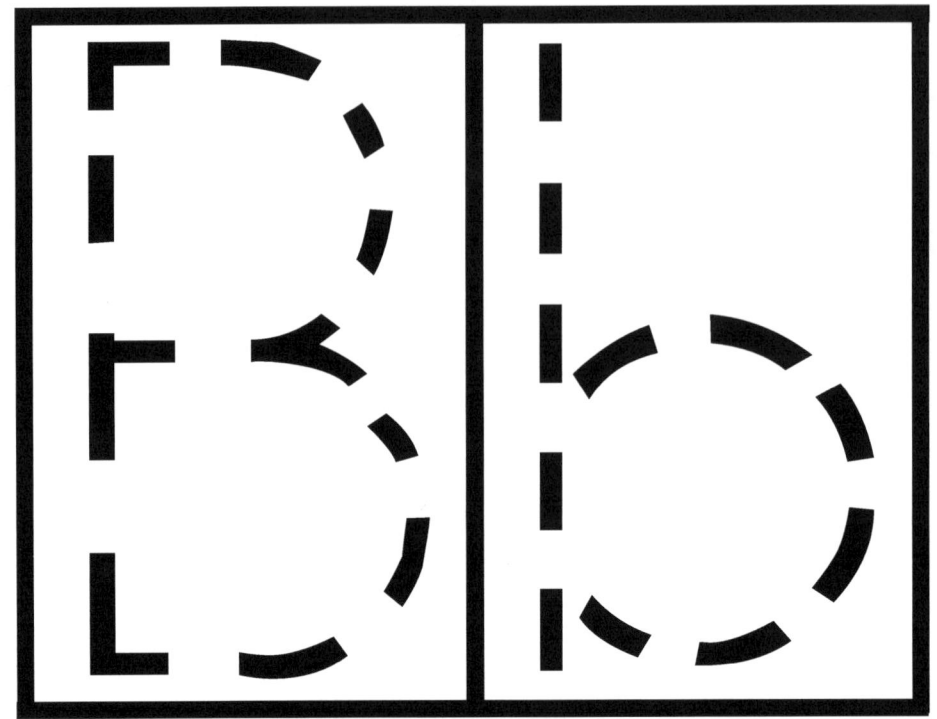

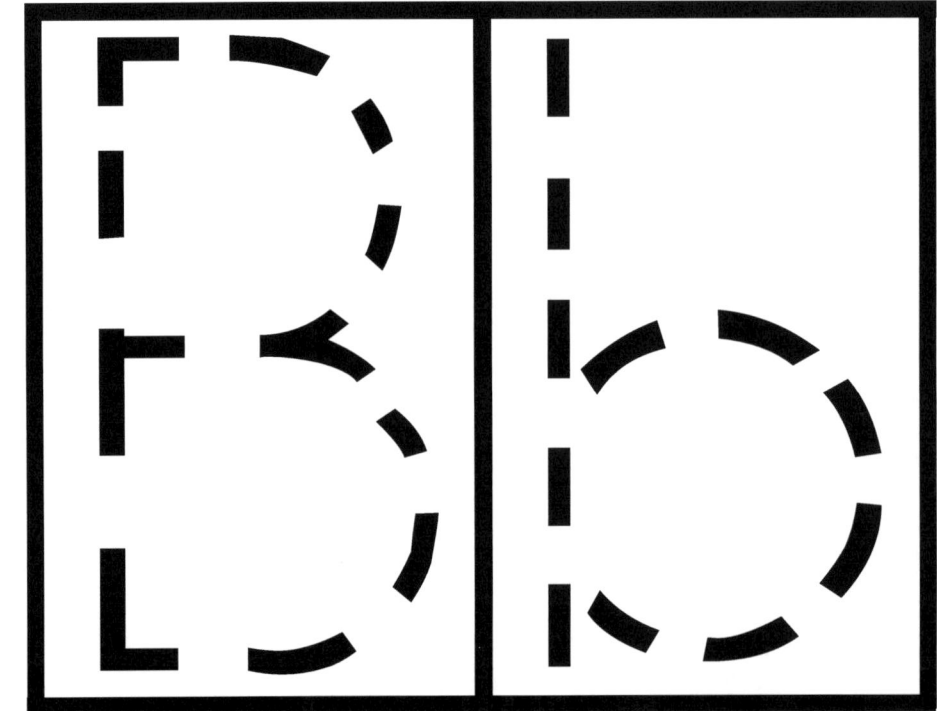

C is for chick. Color the chick.

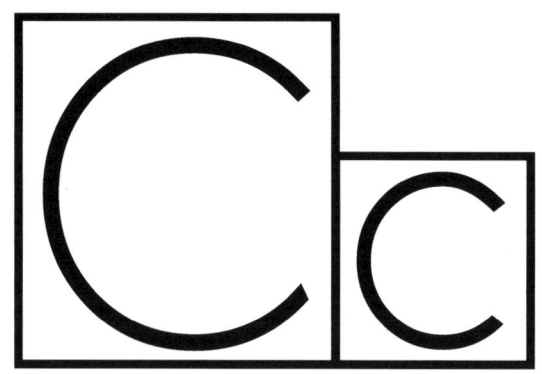

chick

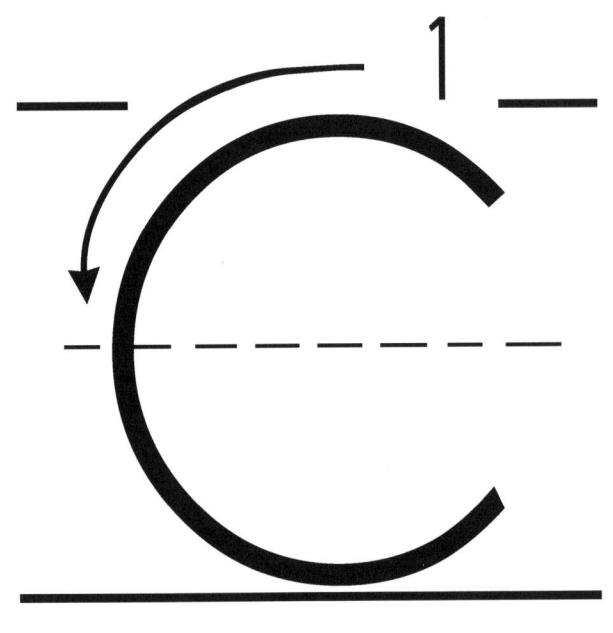

1

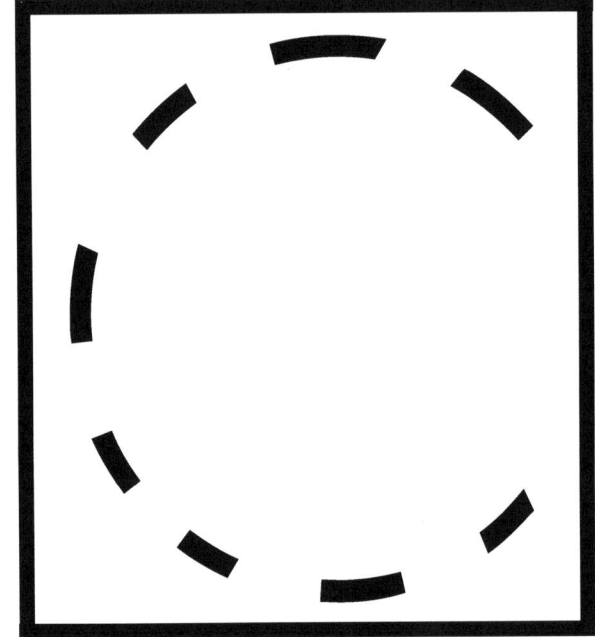

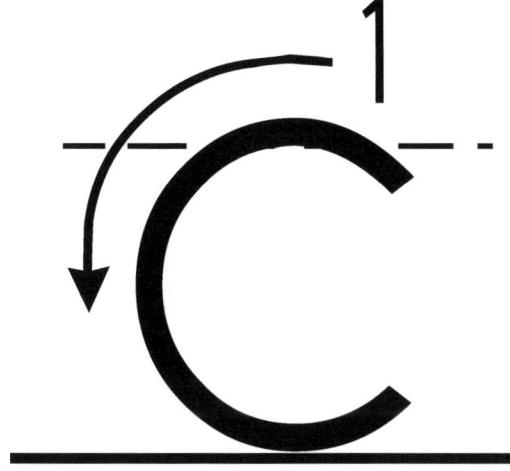

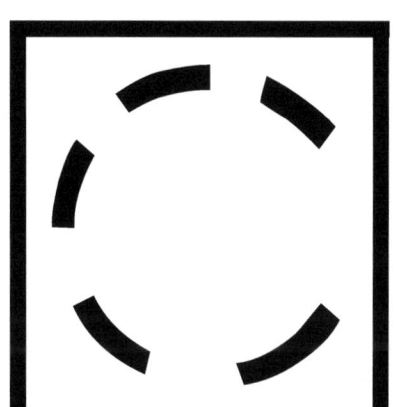

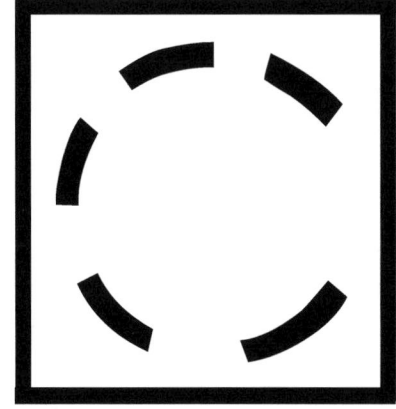

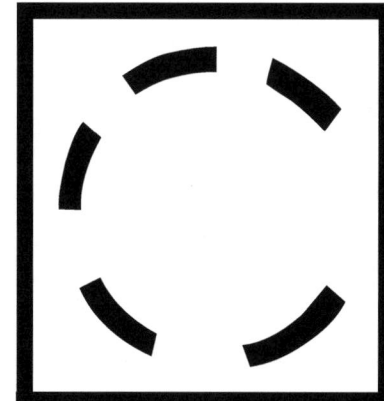

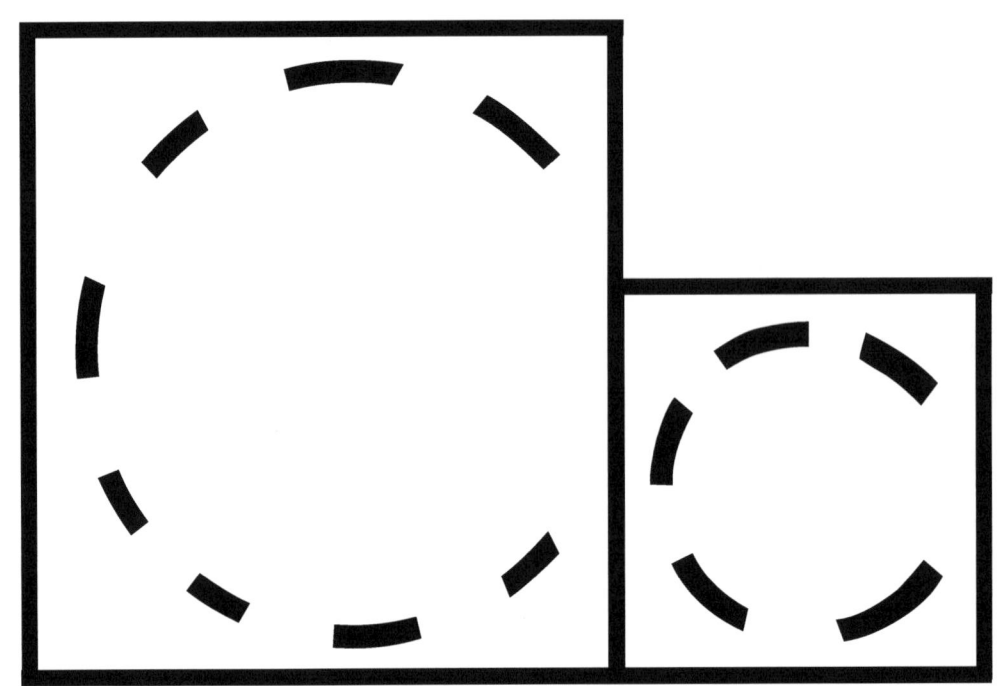

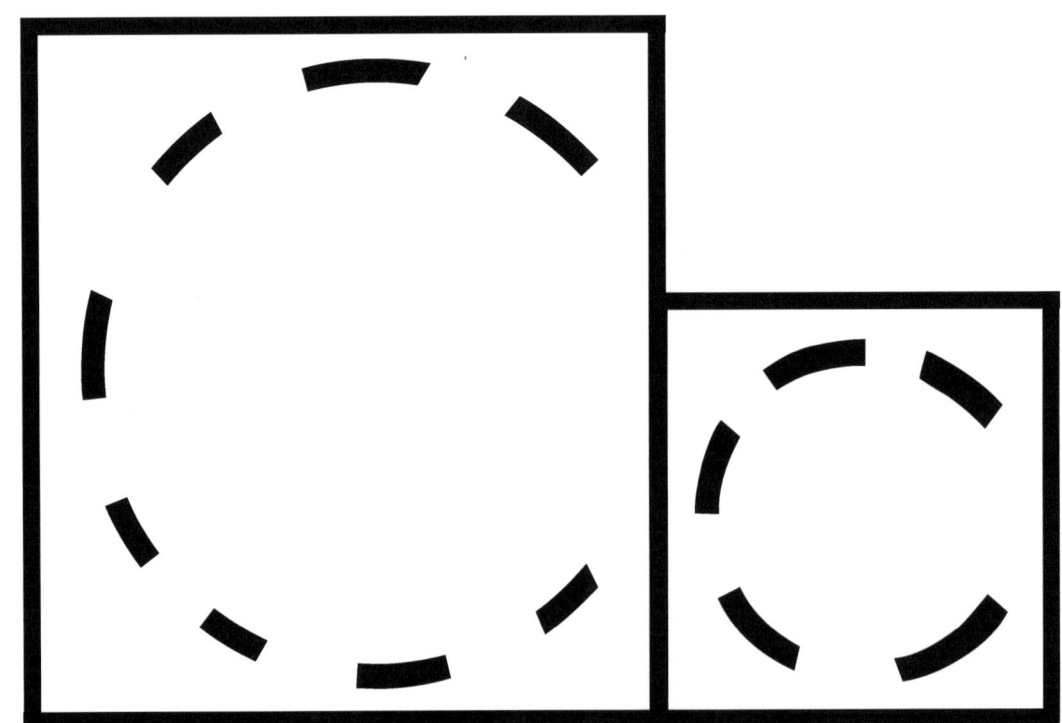

D is for dolphin. Color the dolphin.

dolphin

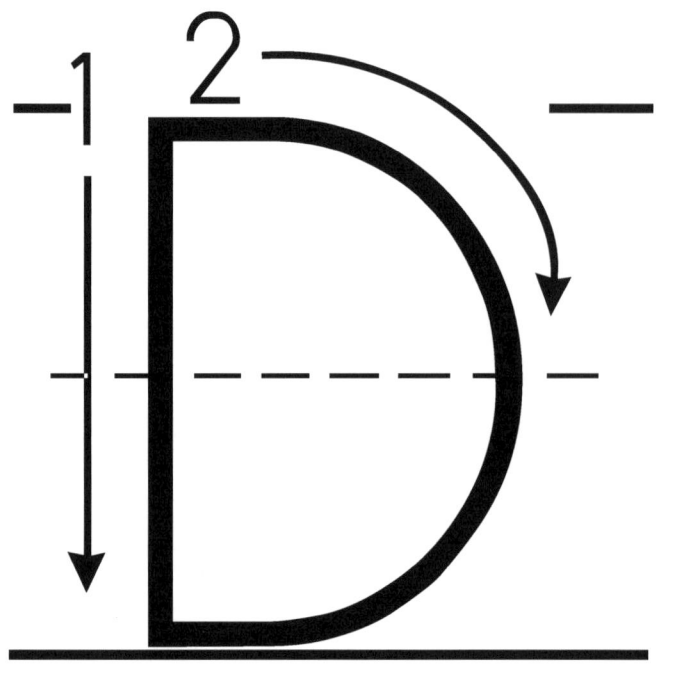

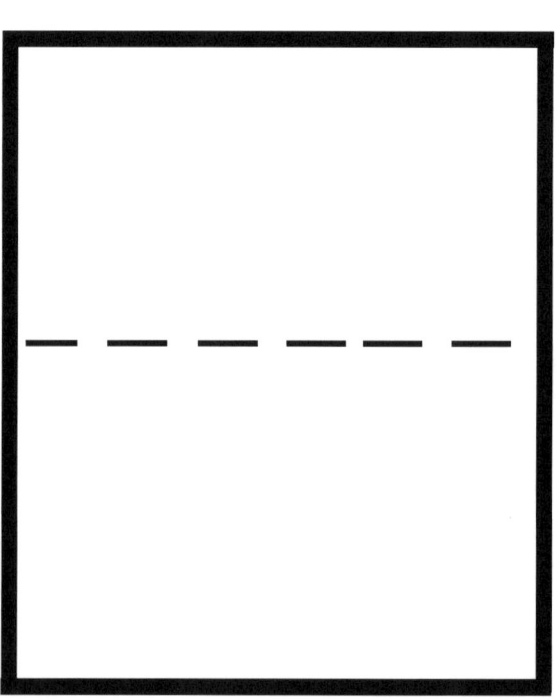

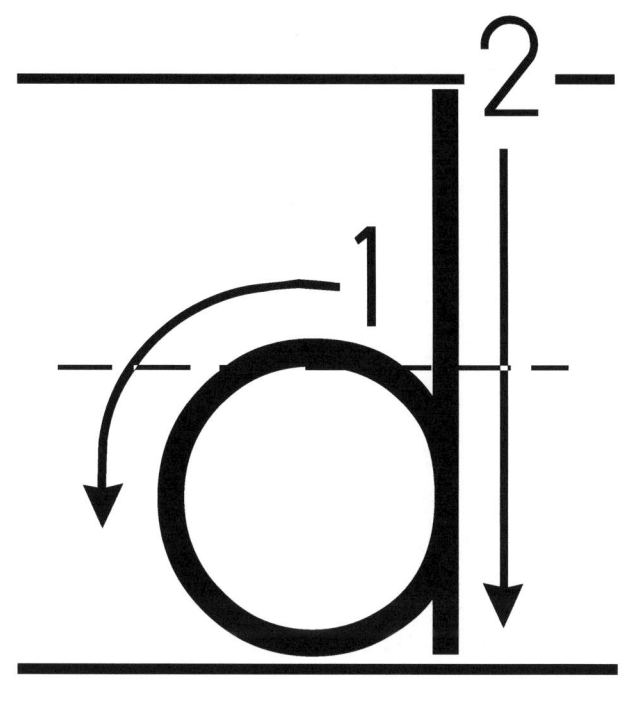

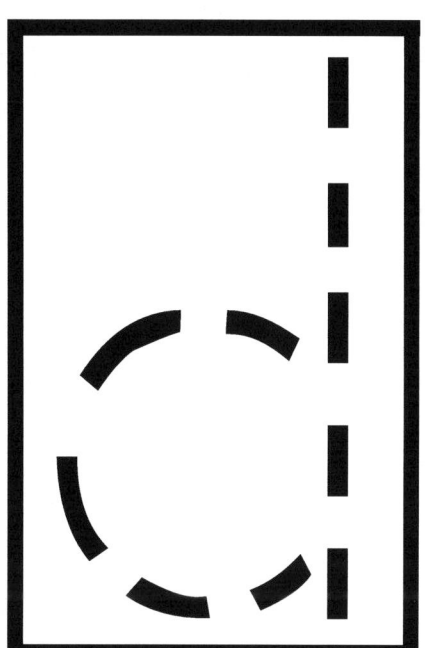

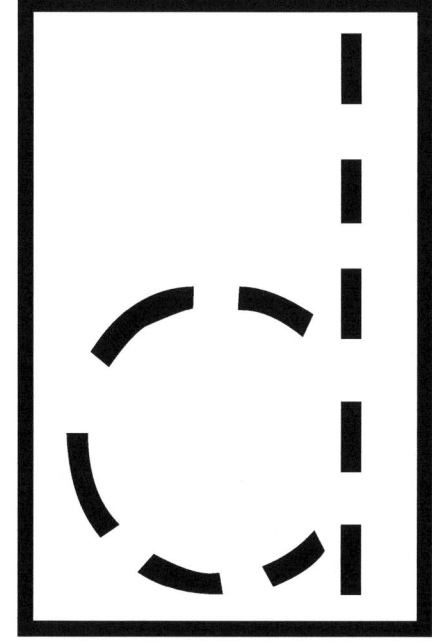

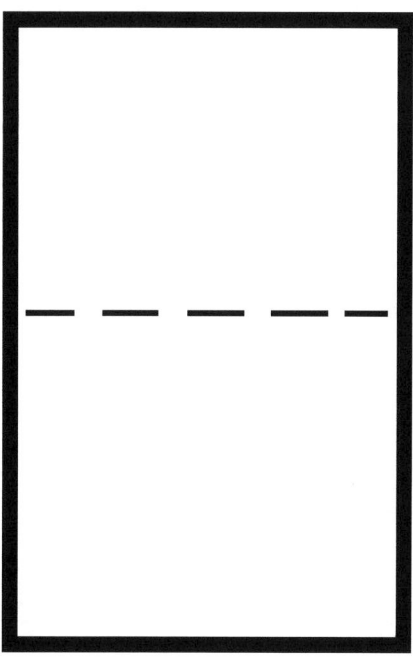

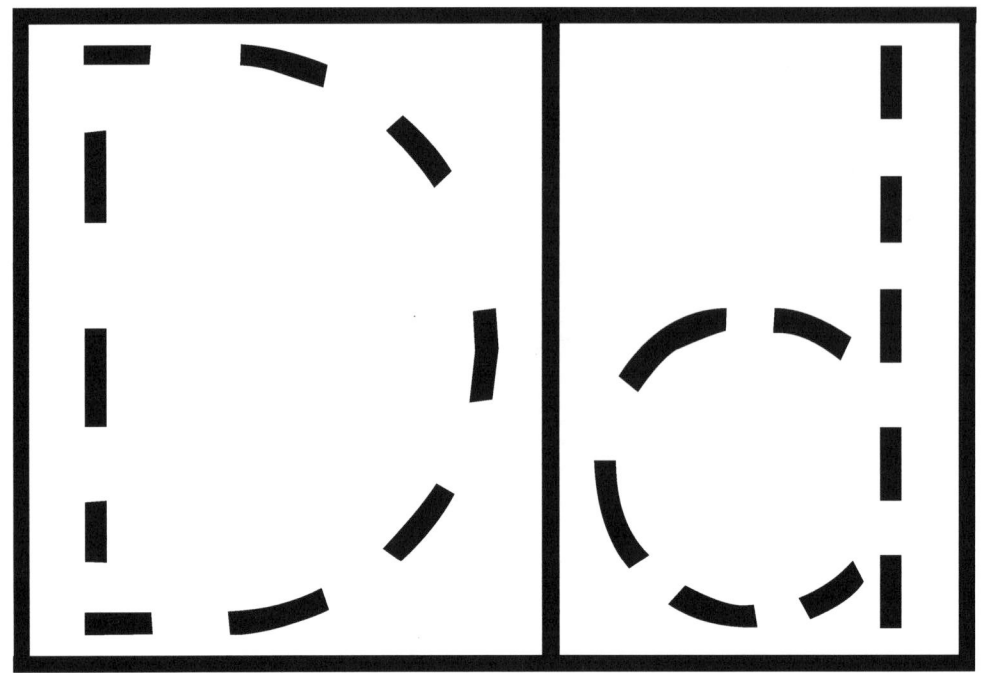

E is for elephant. Color the elephant.

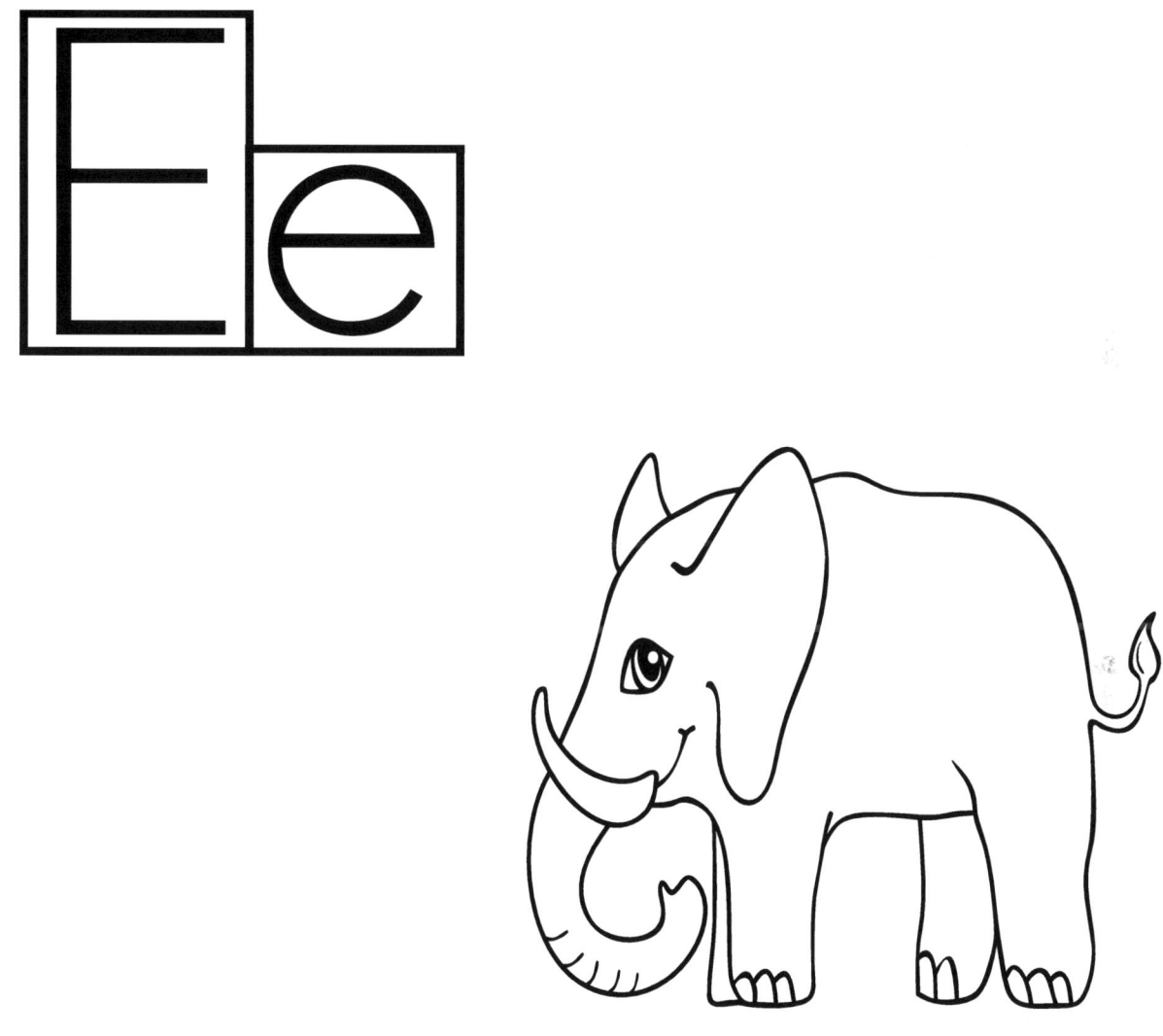

elephant

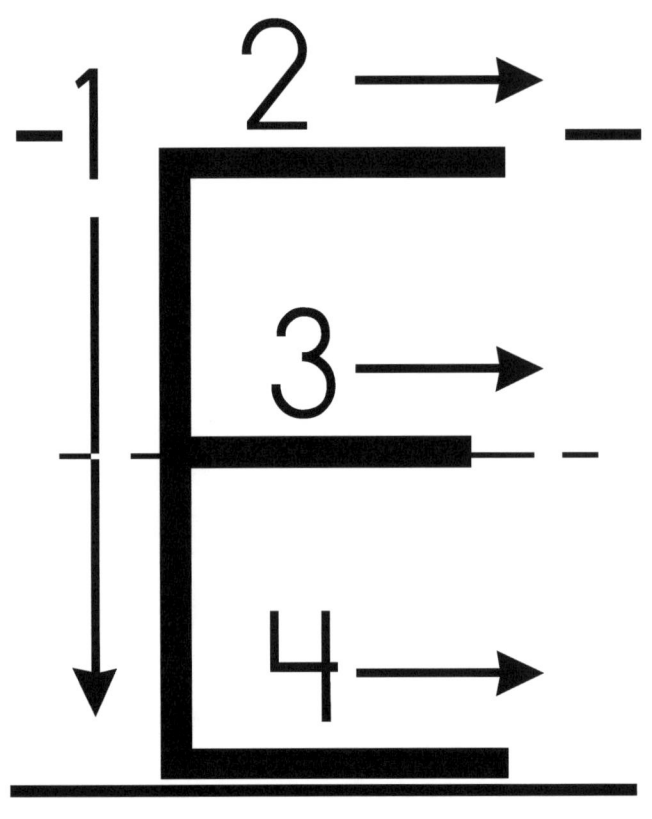
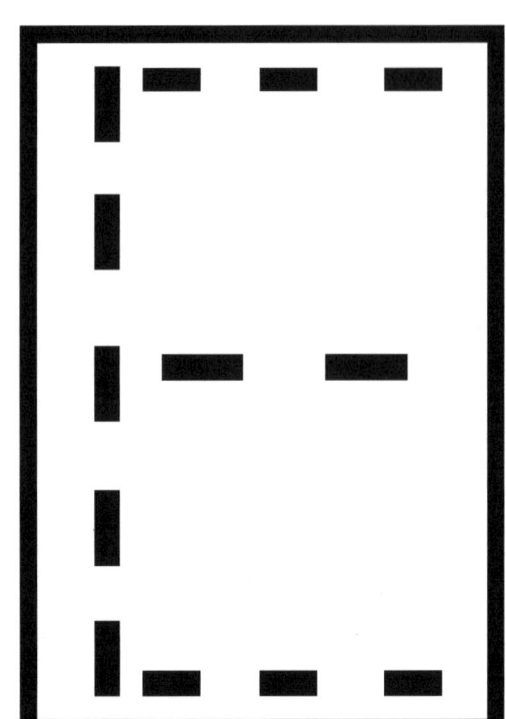
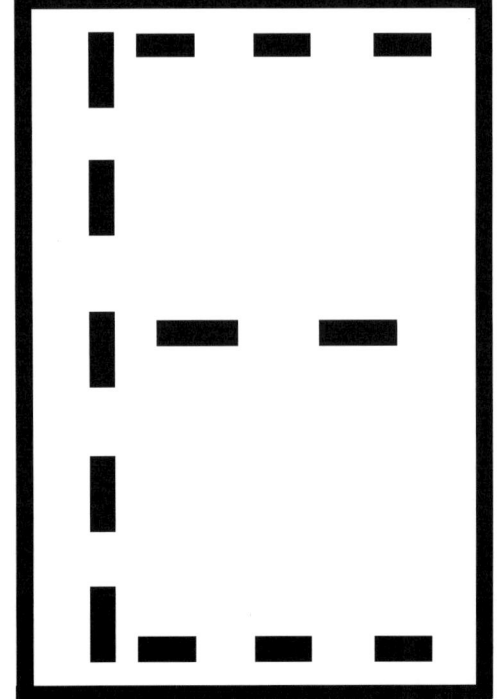
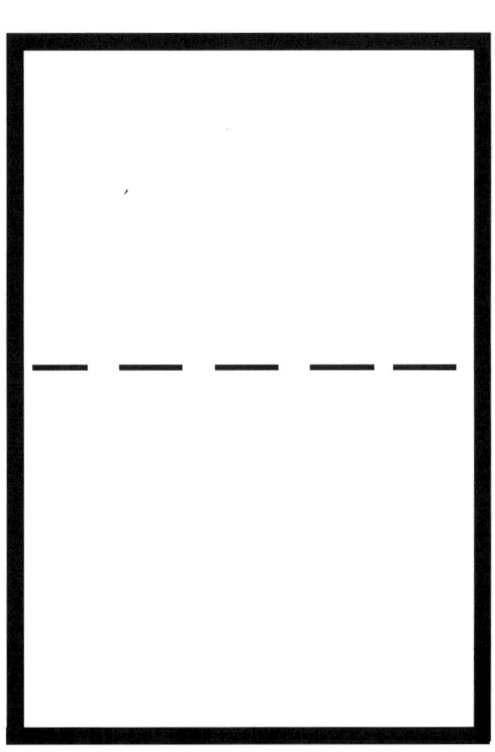

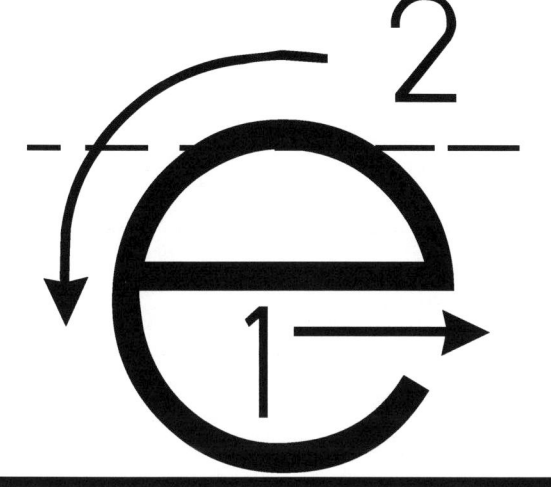

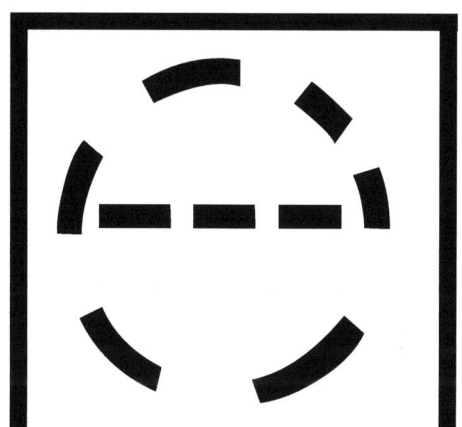

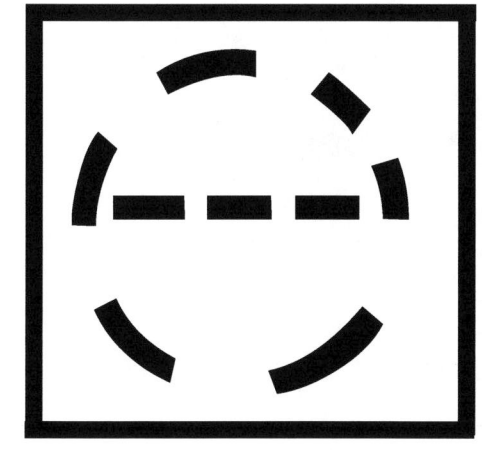

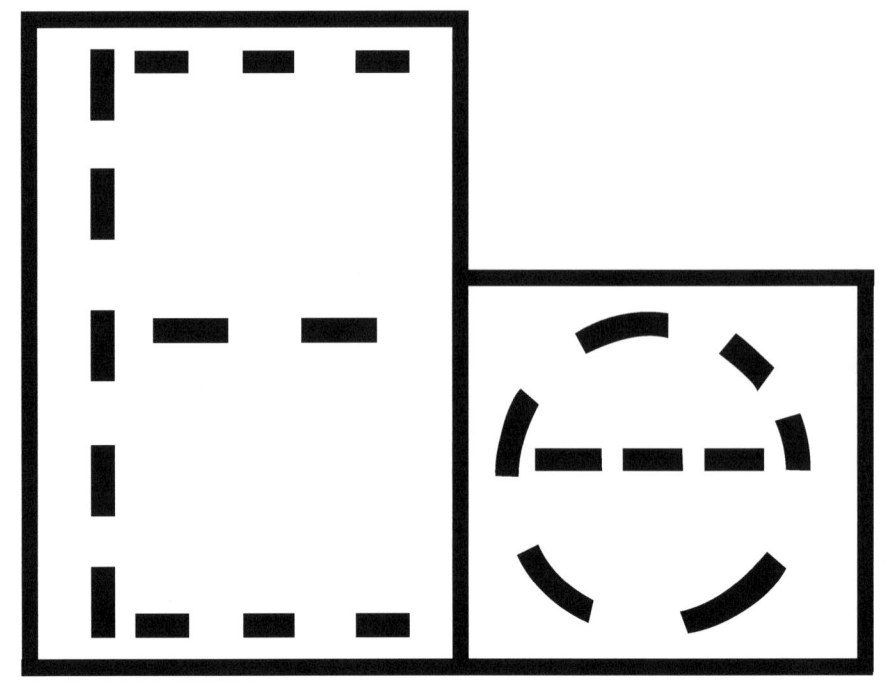

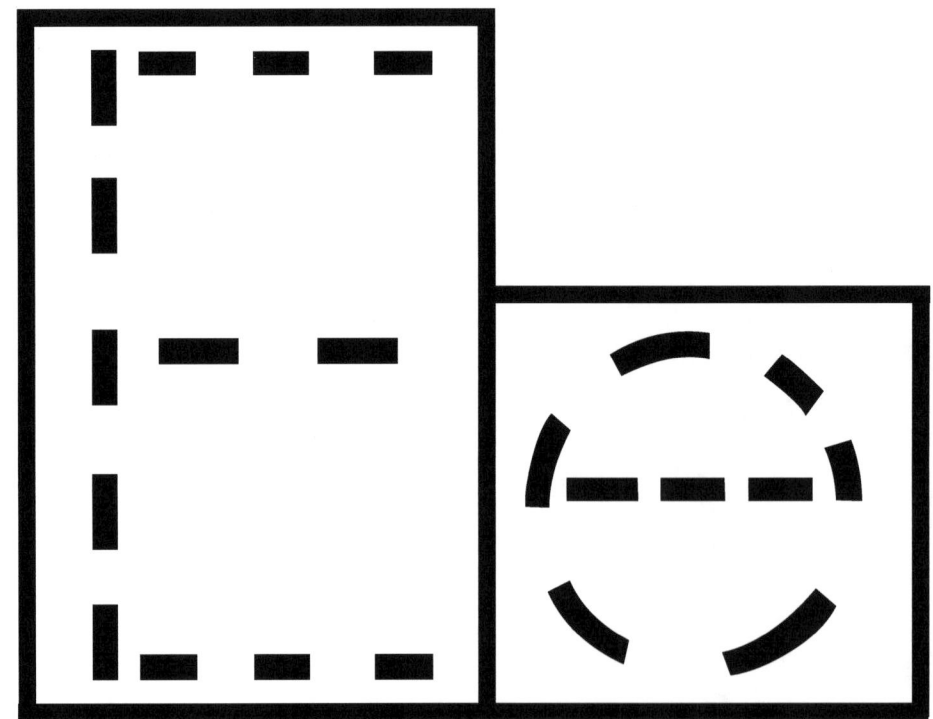

F is for frog. Color the frog.

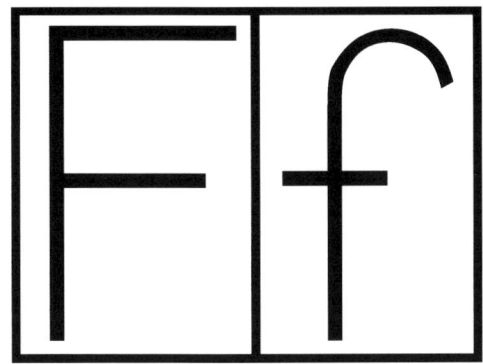

frog

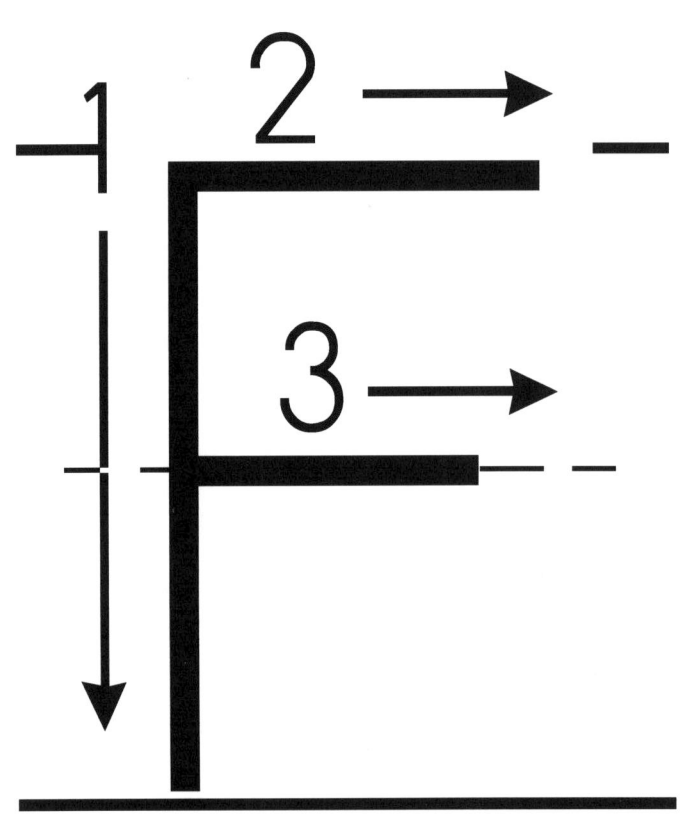

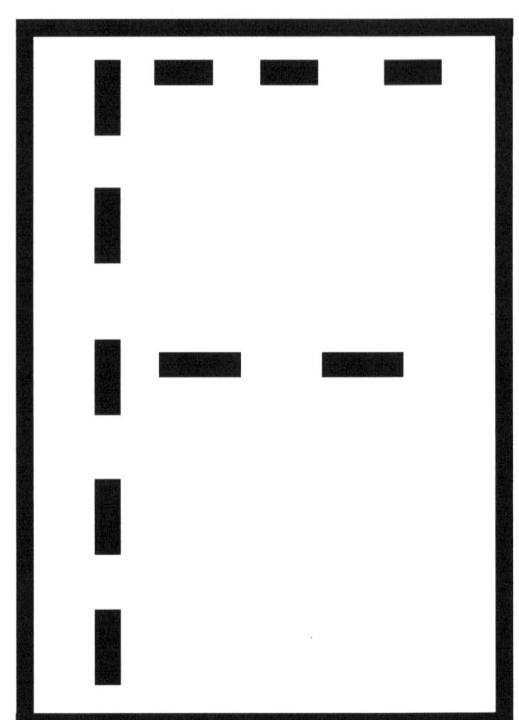

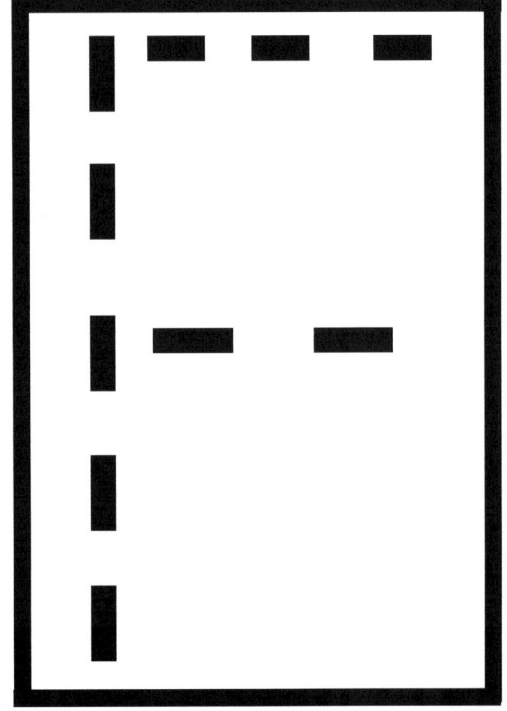

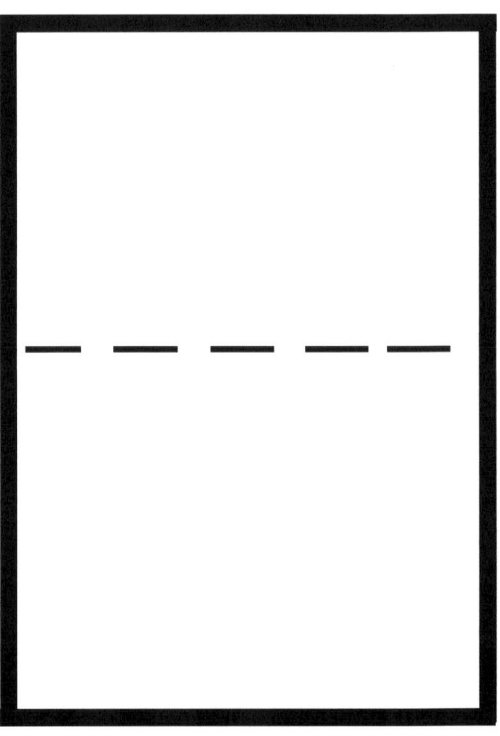

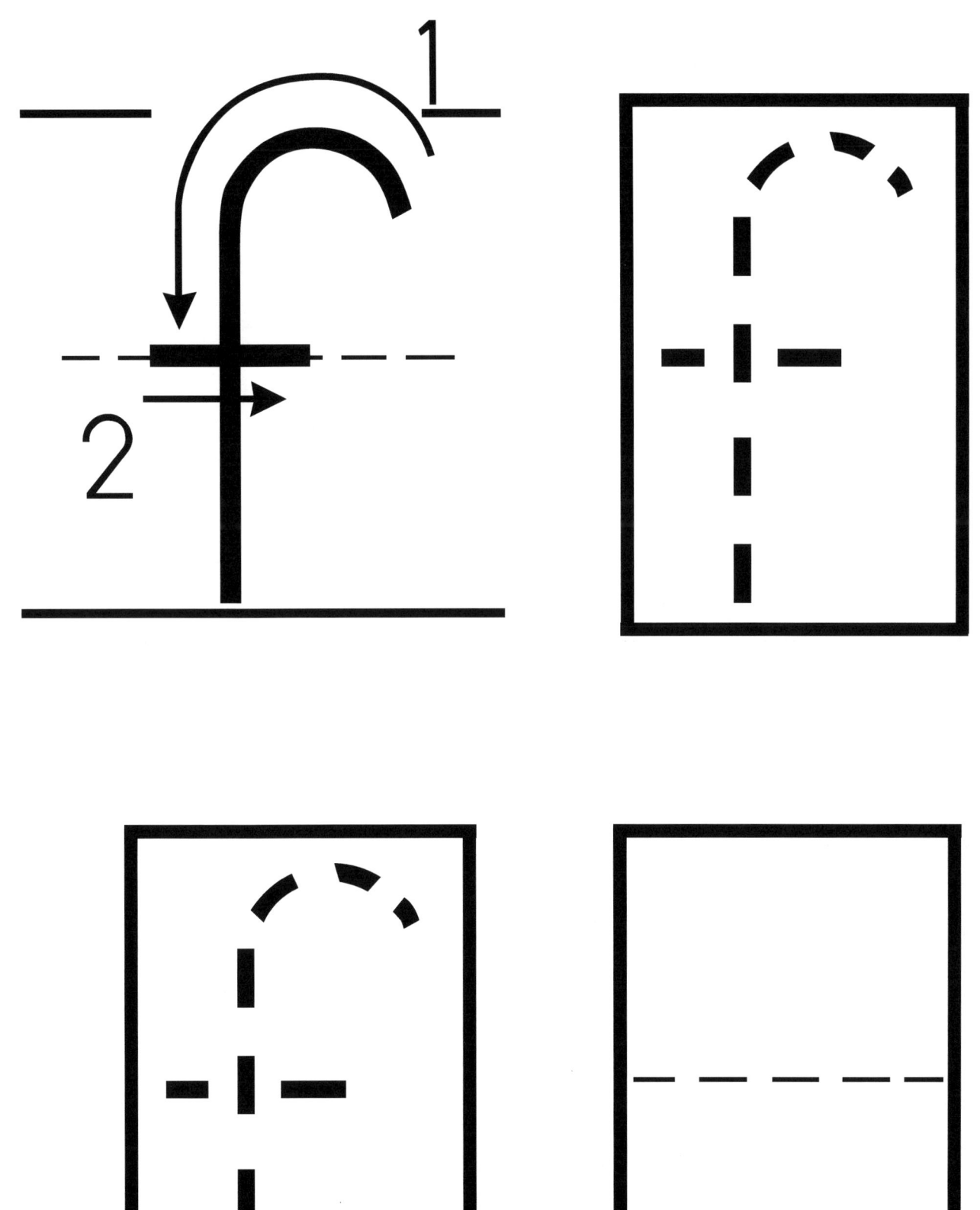

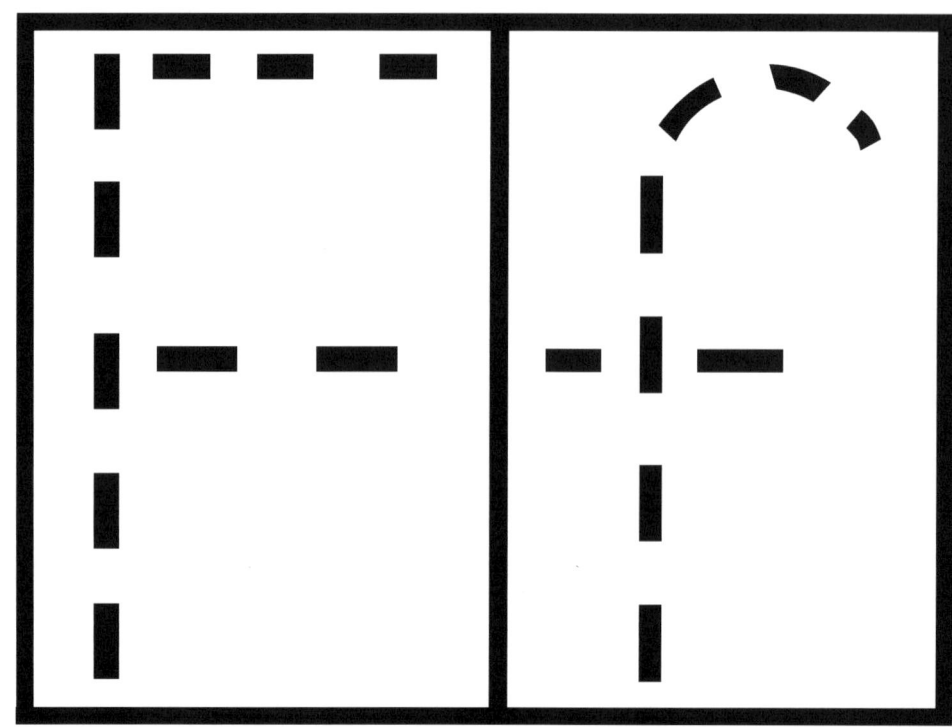

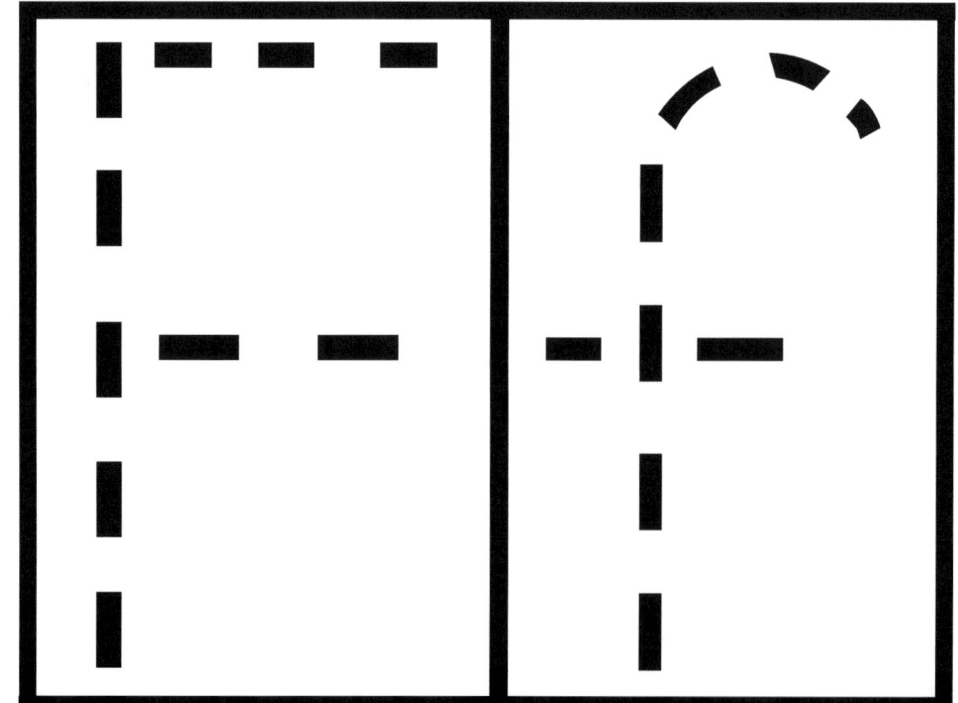

G is for giraffe. Color the giraffe.

giraffe

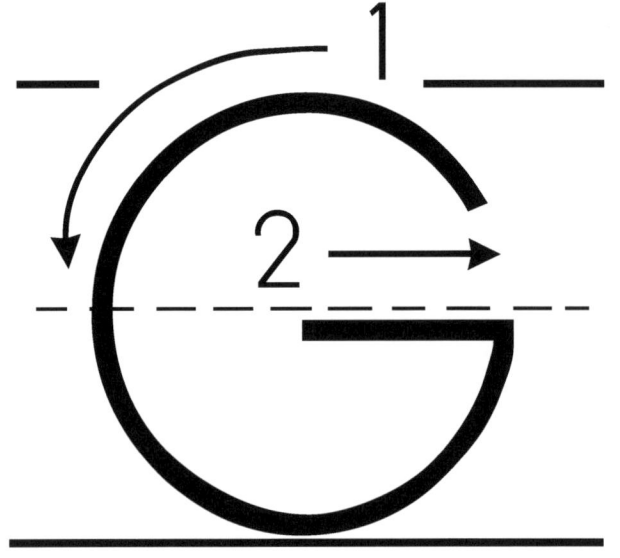
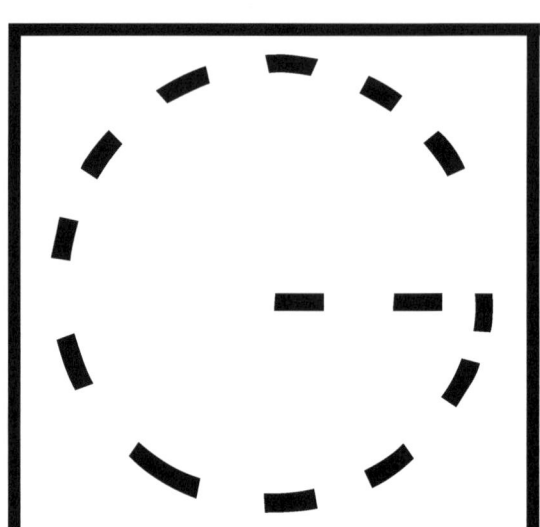
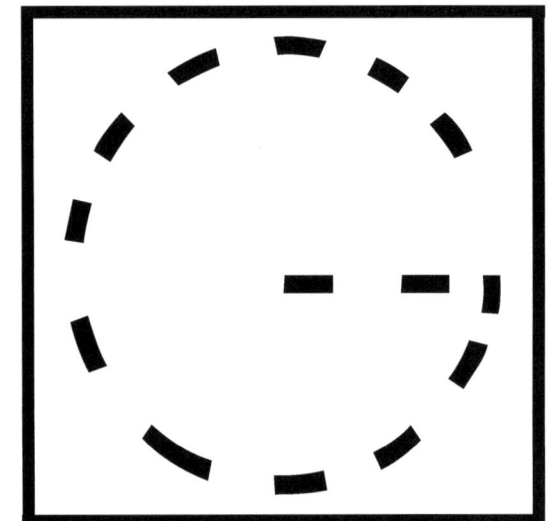
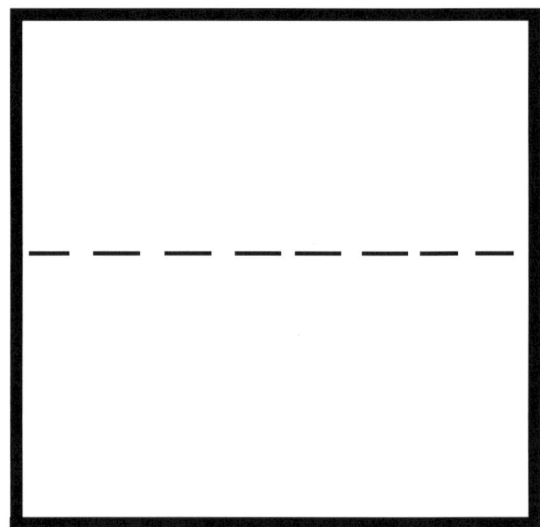

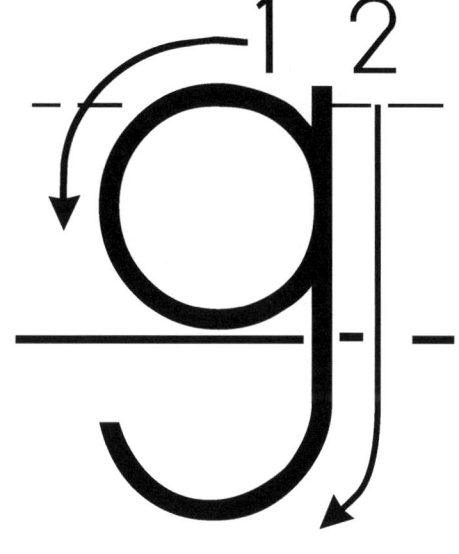

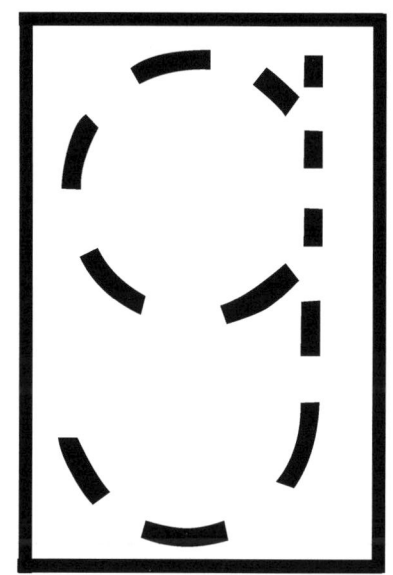

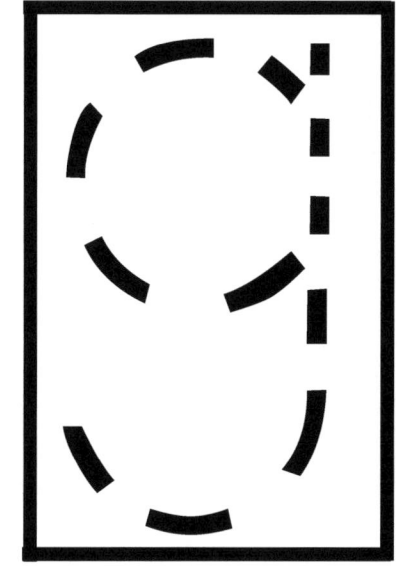

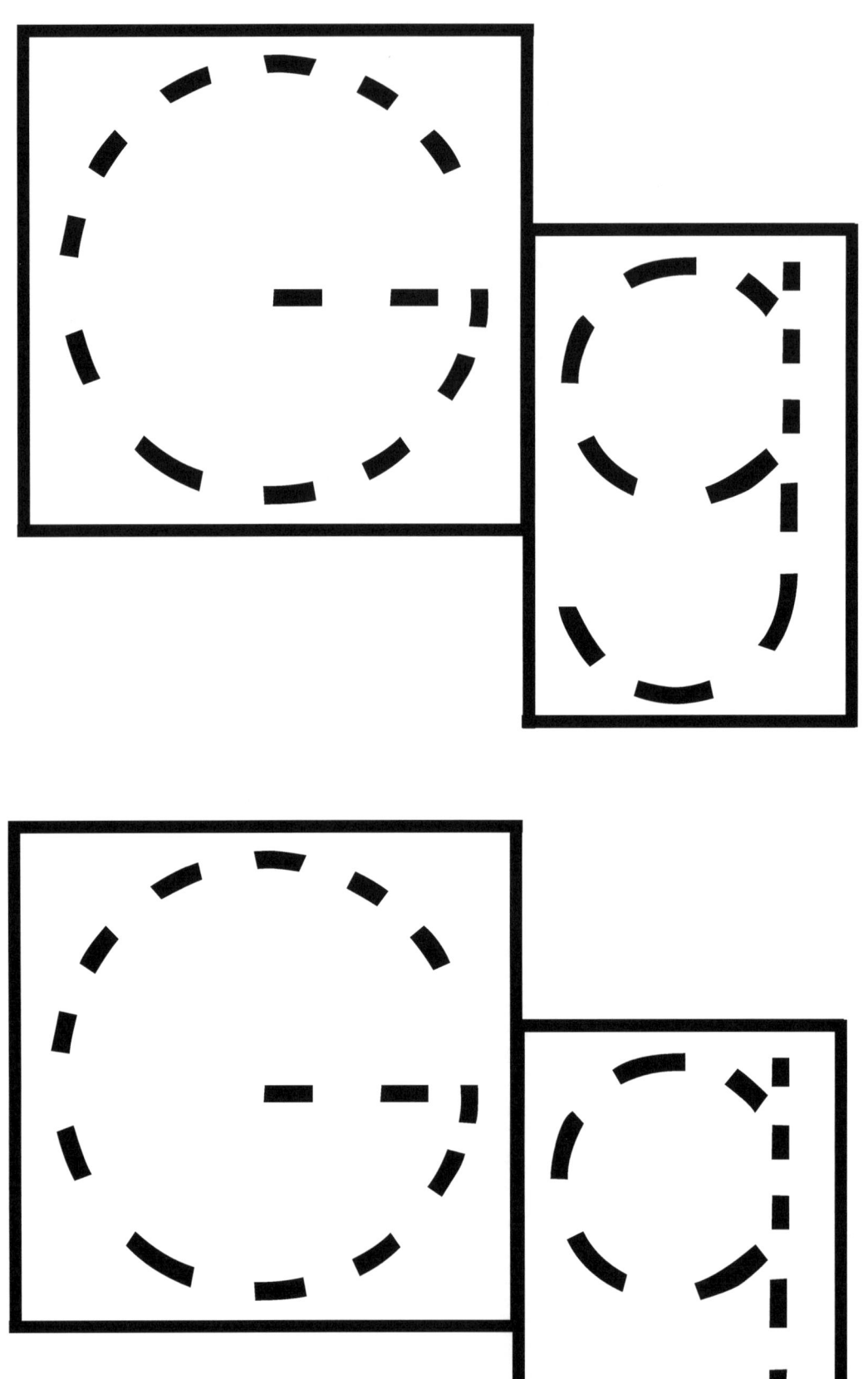

H is for hedgehog. Color the hedgehog.

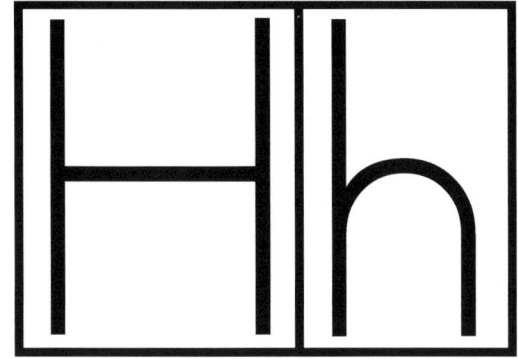

hedgehog

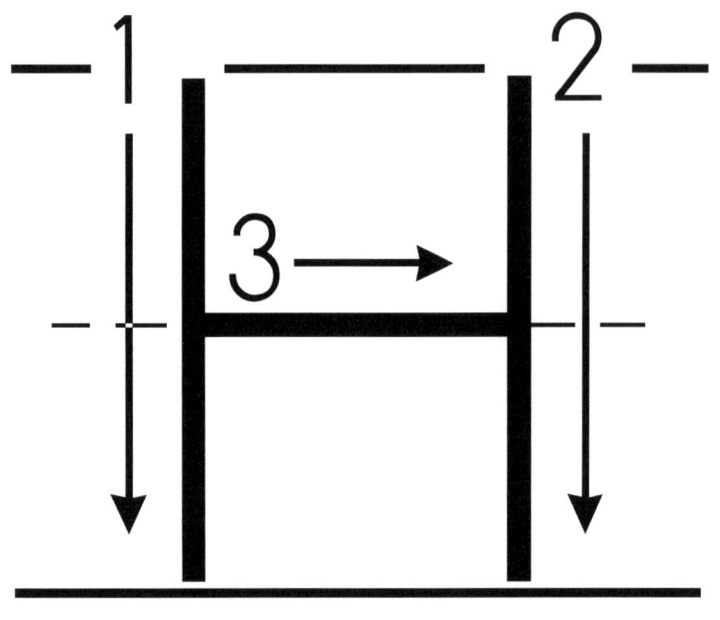

1 2

3 →

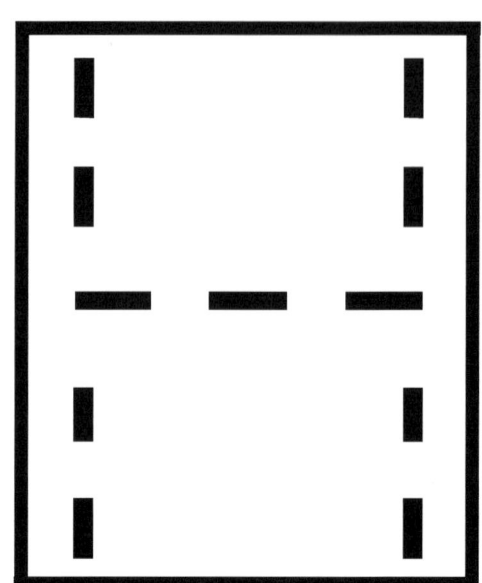

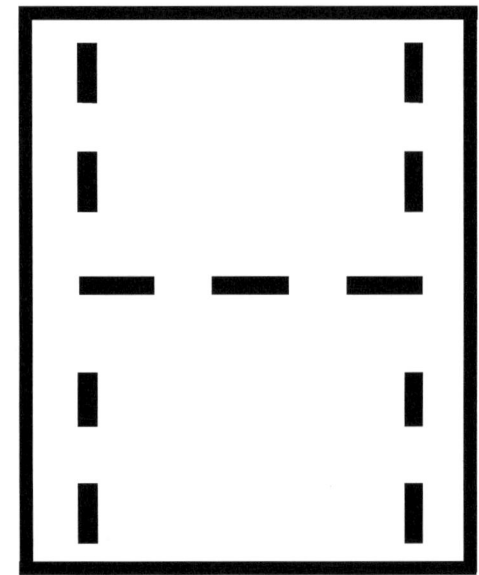

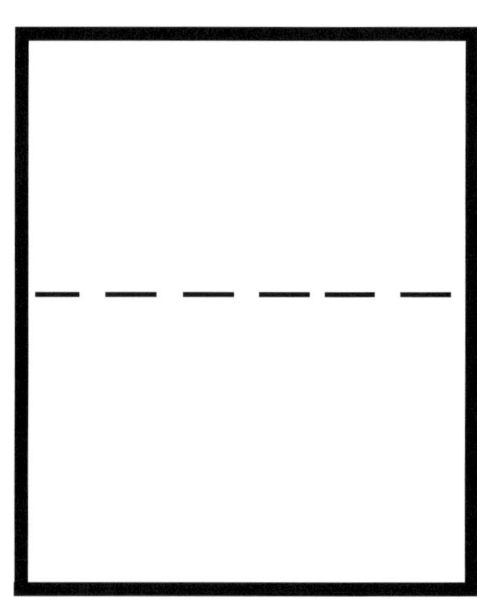

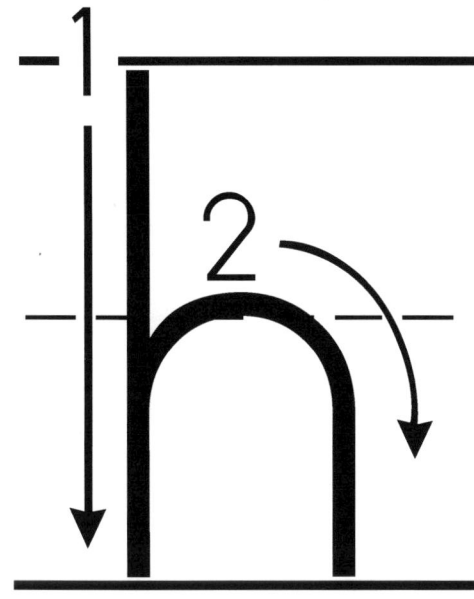
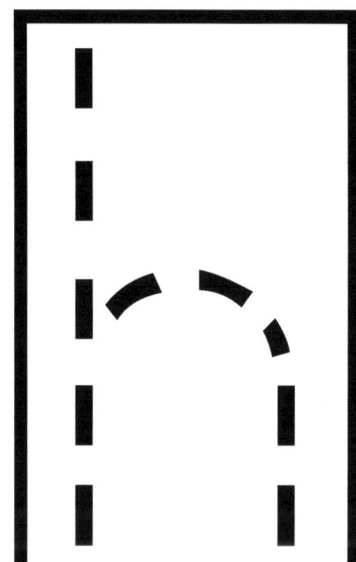
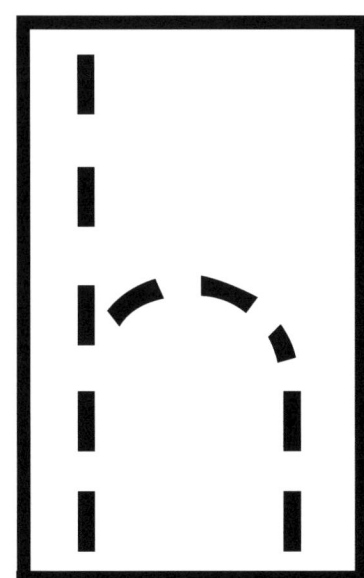
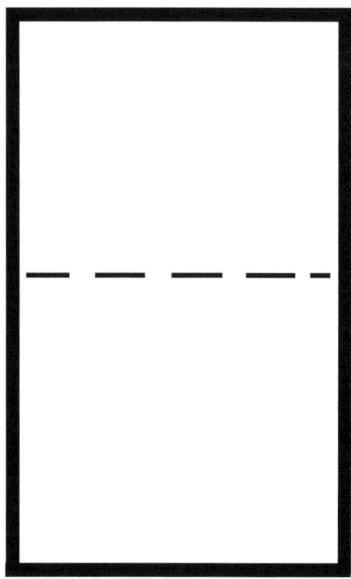

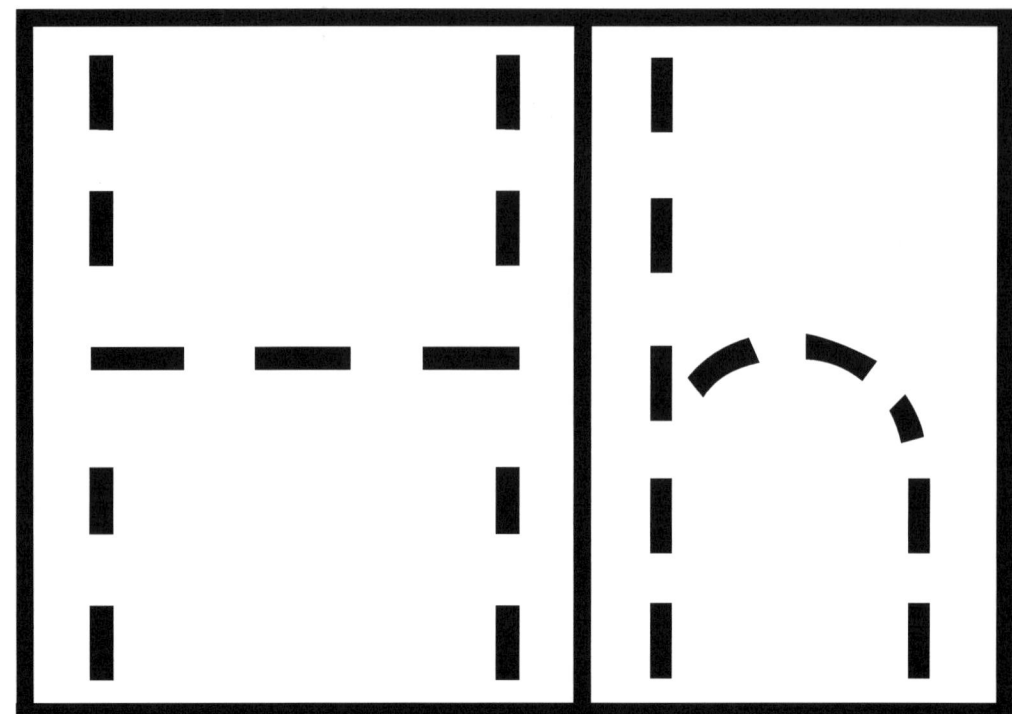

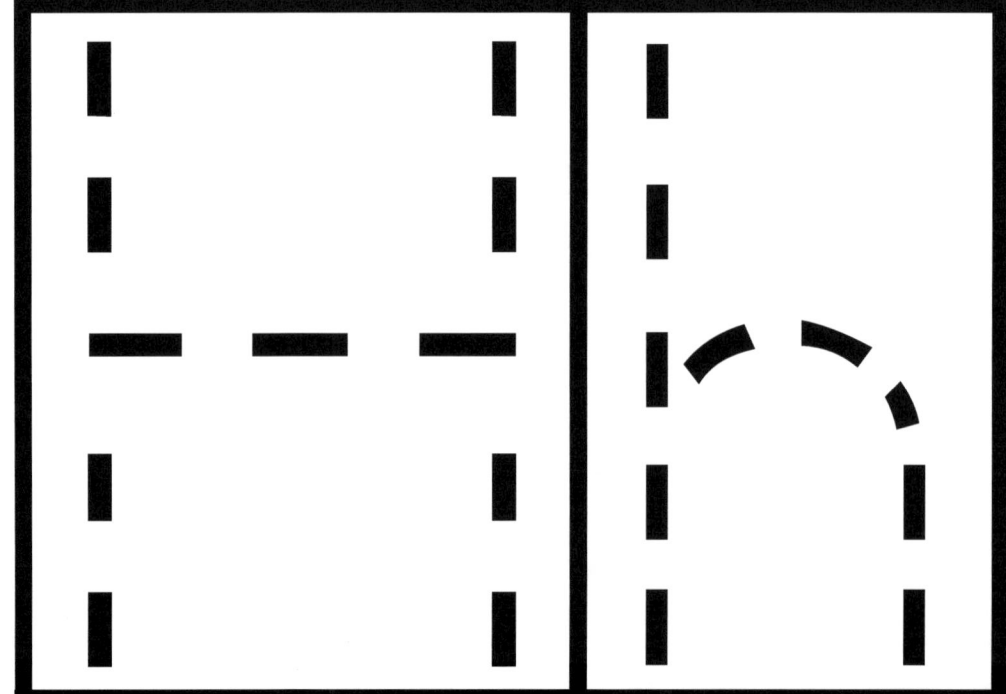

I is for ibis. Color the ibis.

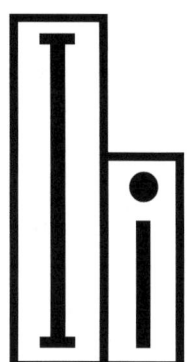

ibis

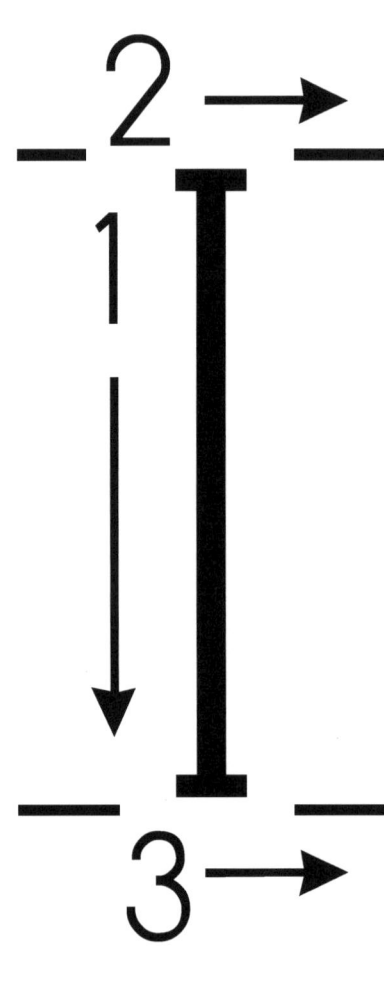

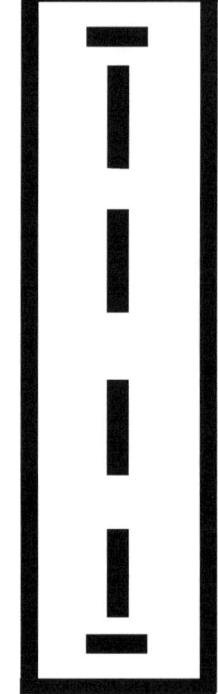

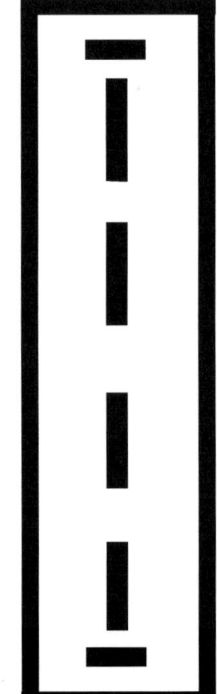

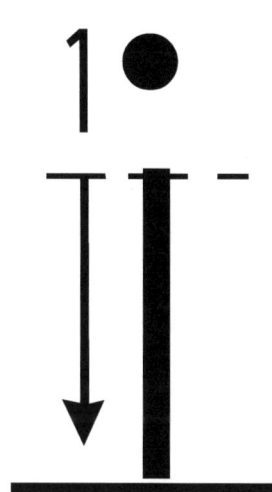

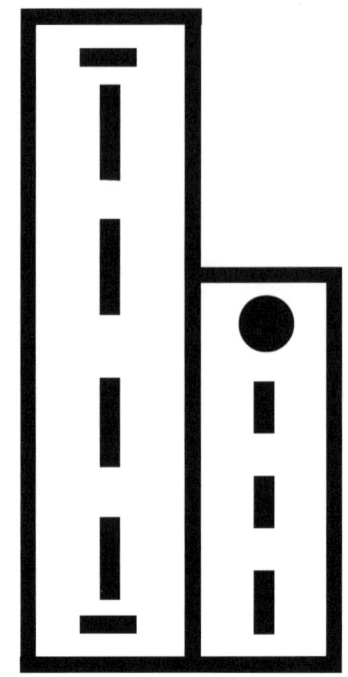

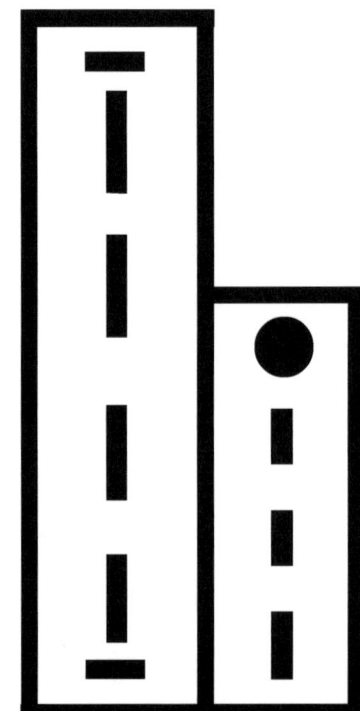

J is for jellyfish. Color the jellyfish.

jellyfish

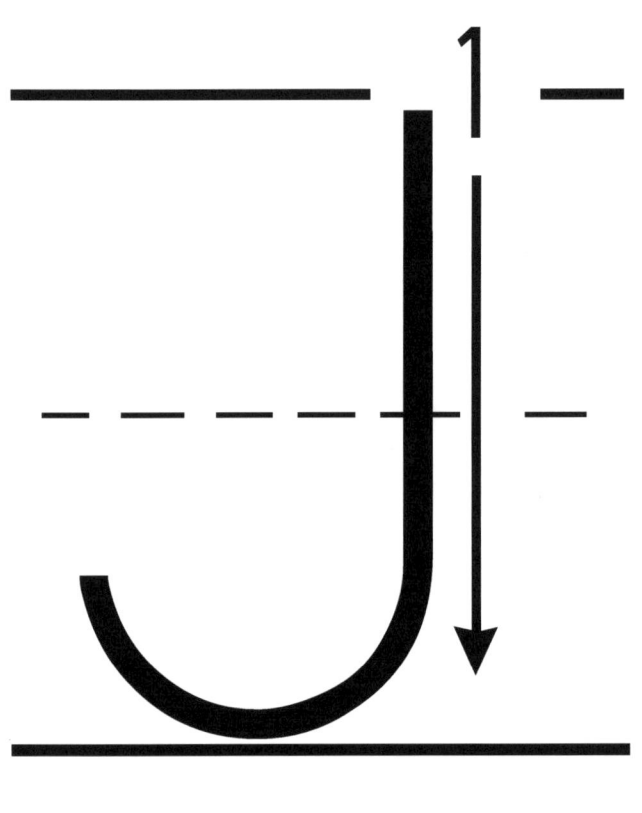

1

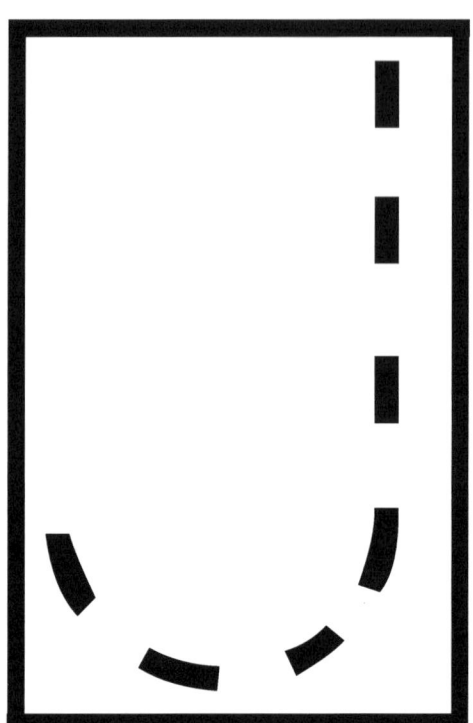

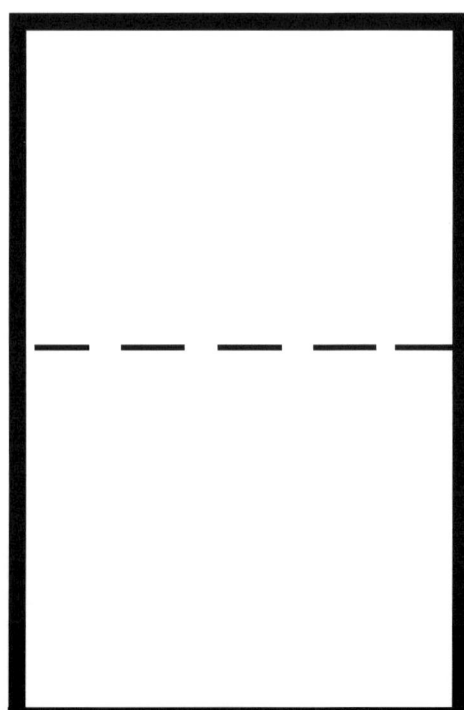

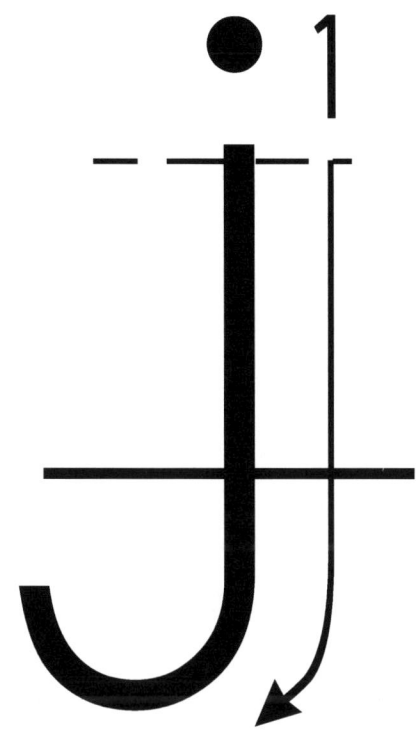

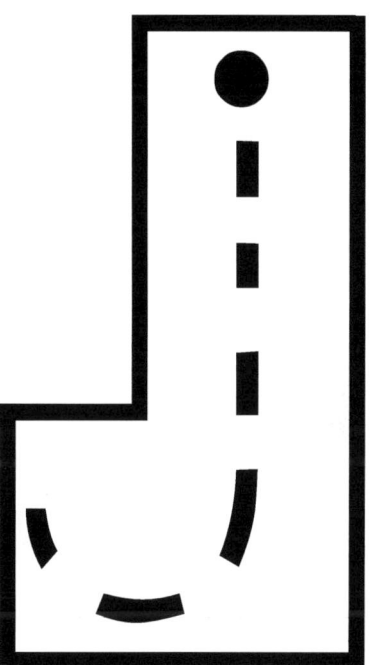

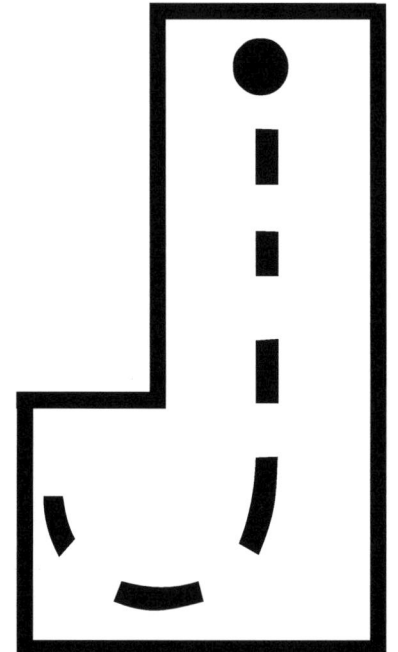

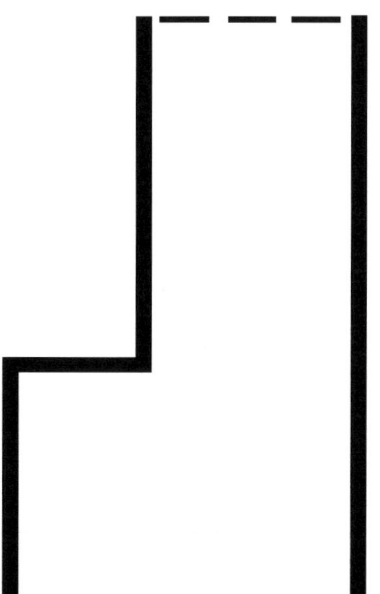

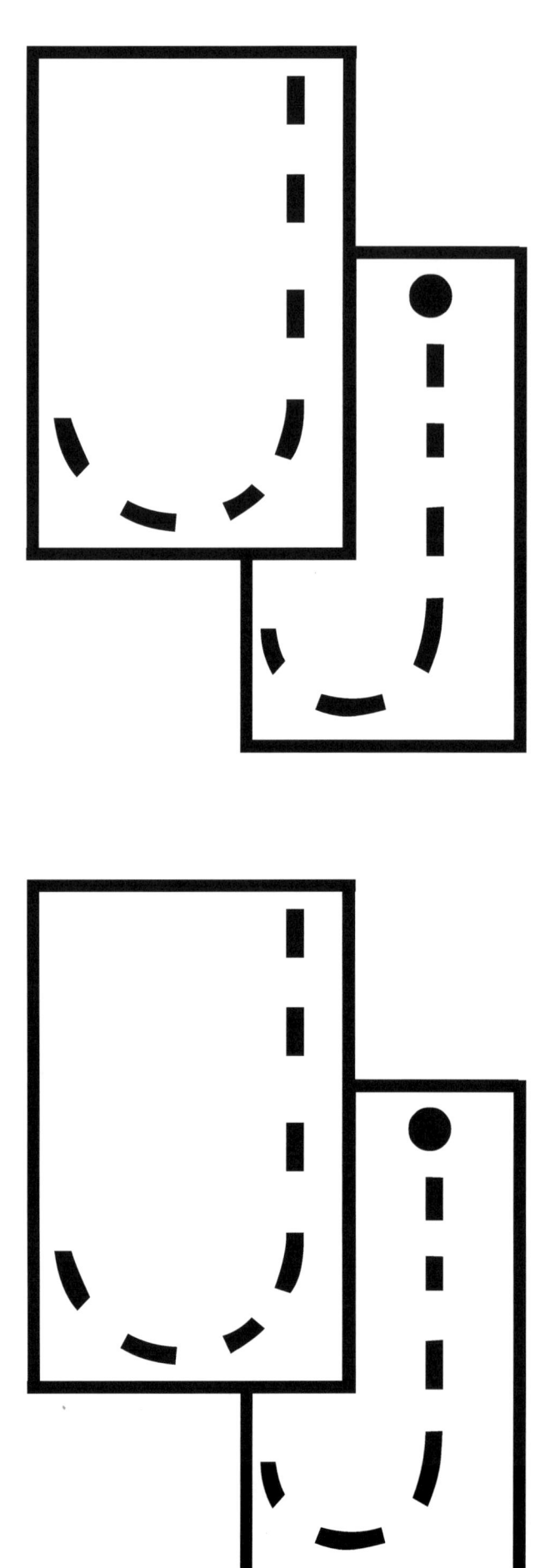

K is for kangaroo. Color the kangaroo.

kangaroo

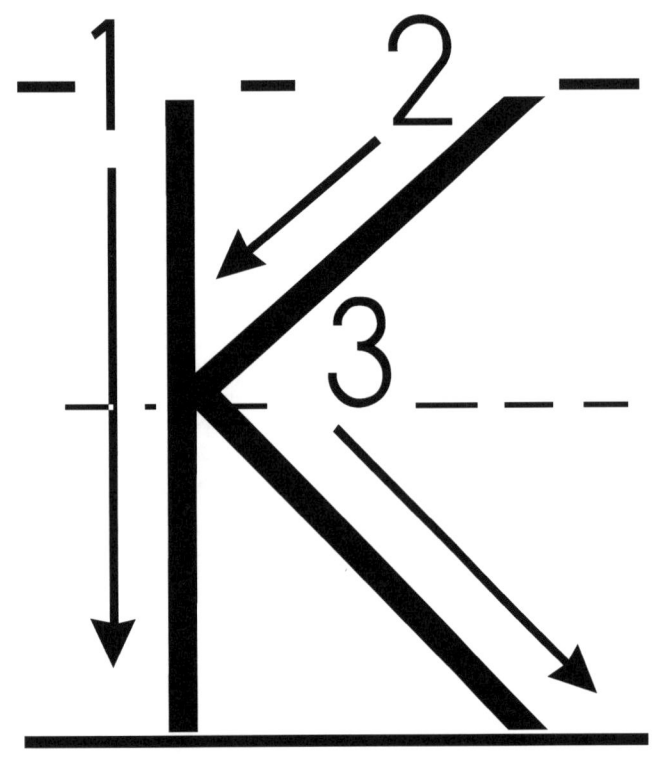

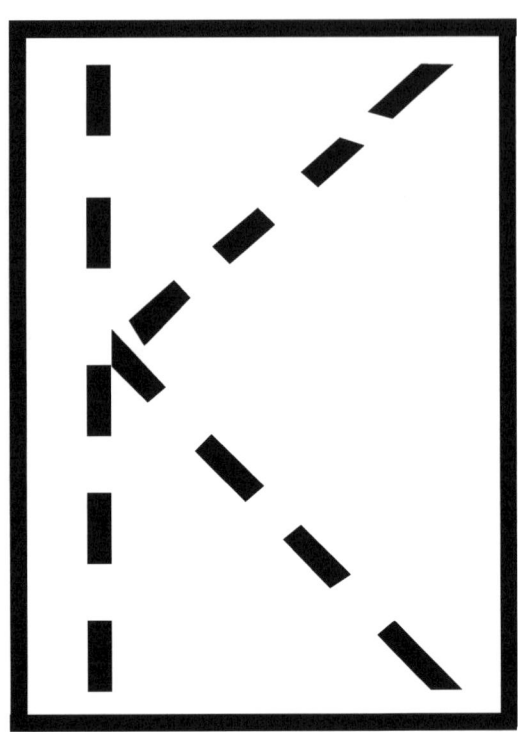

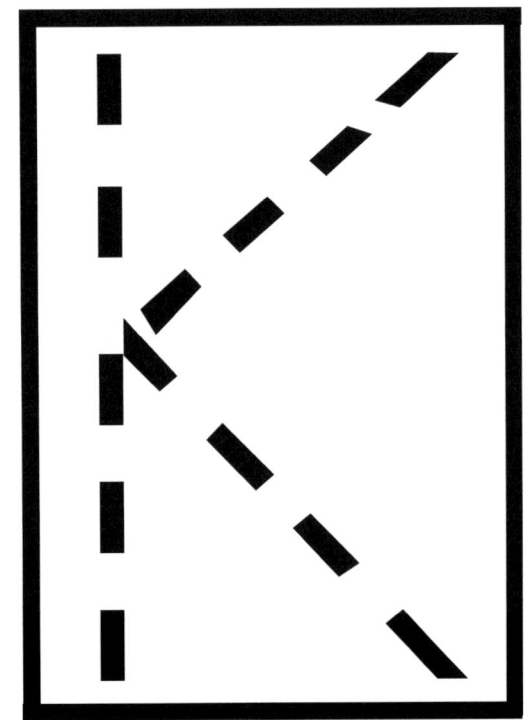

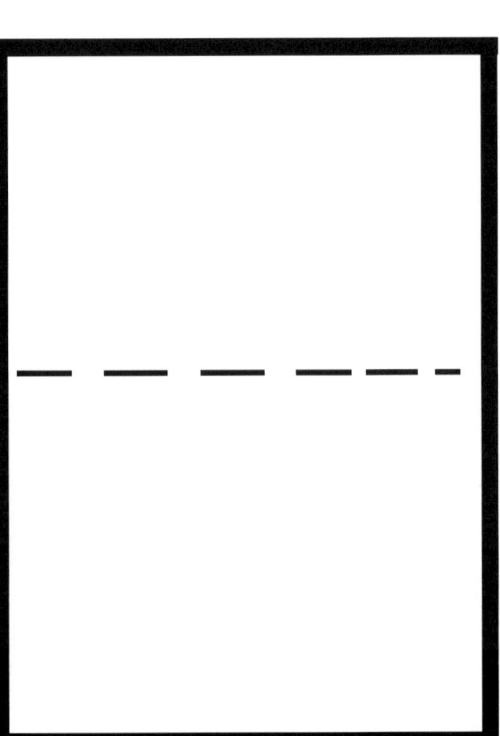

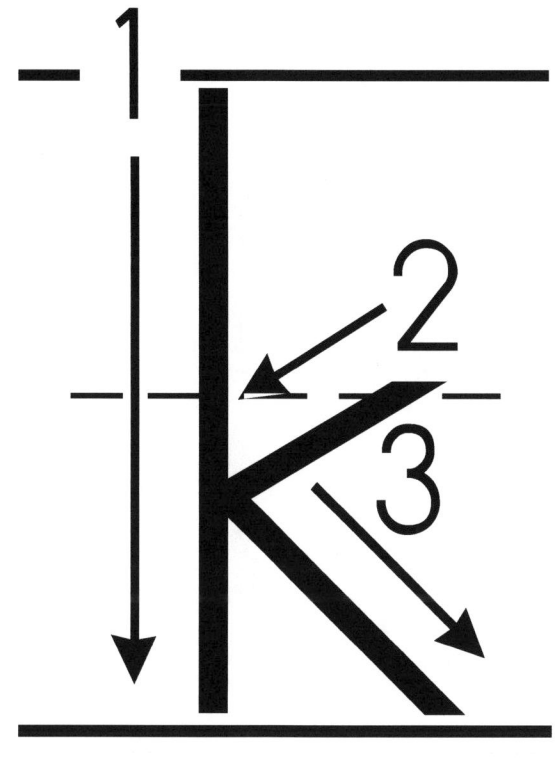

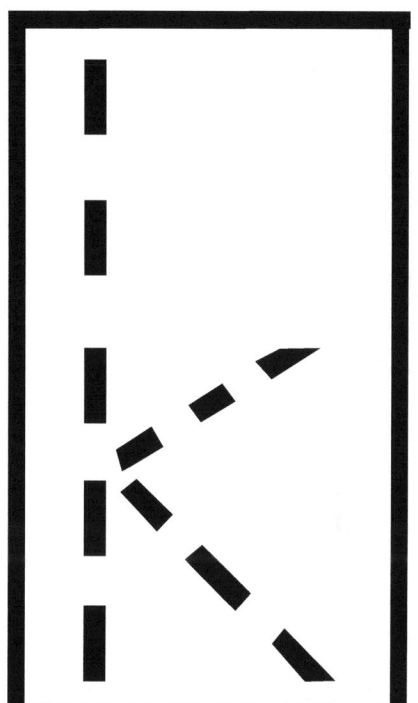

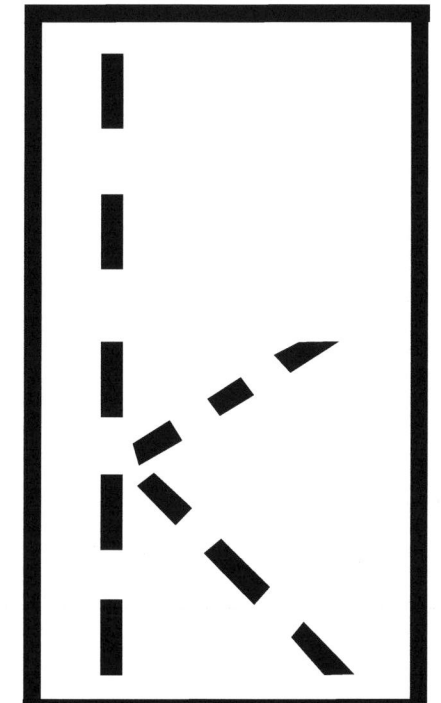

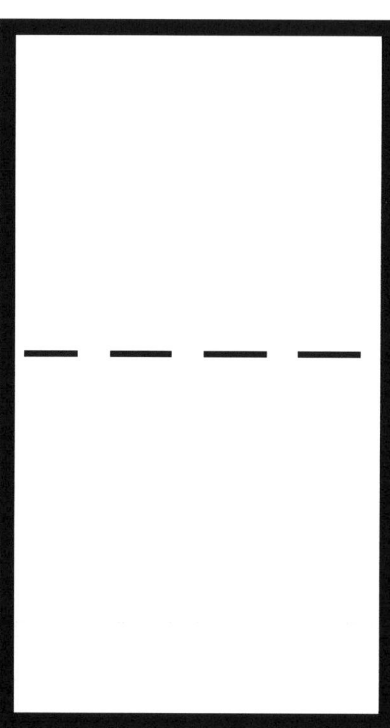

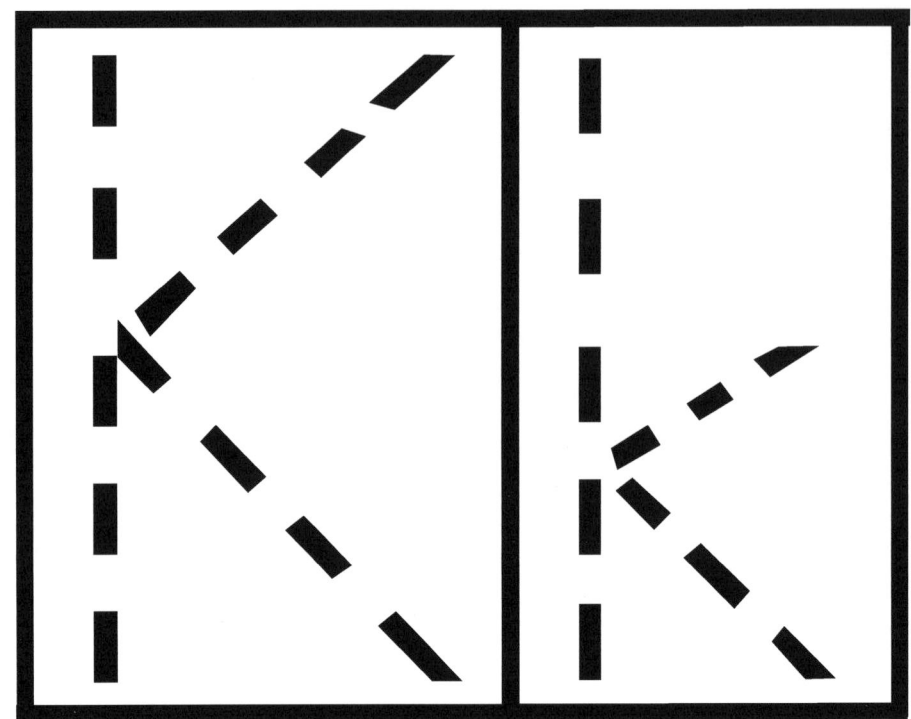

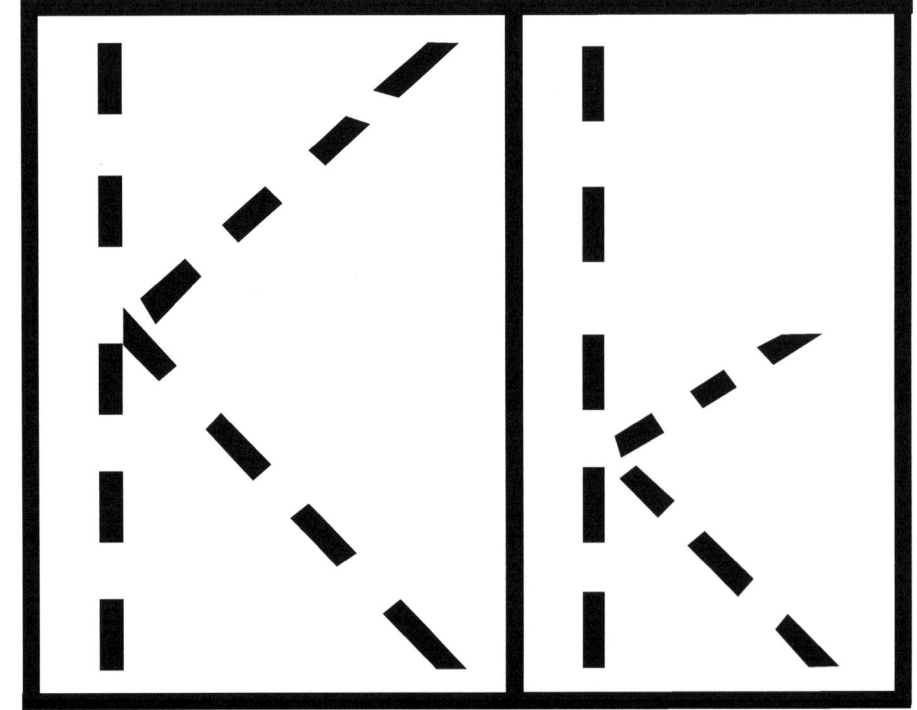

L is for lizard. Color the lizard.

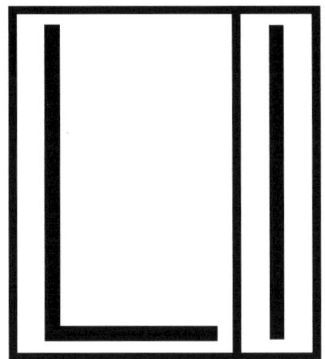

lizard

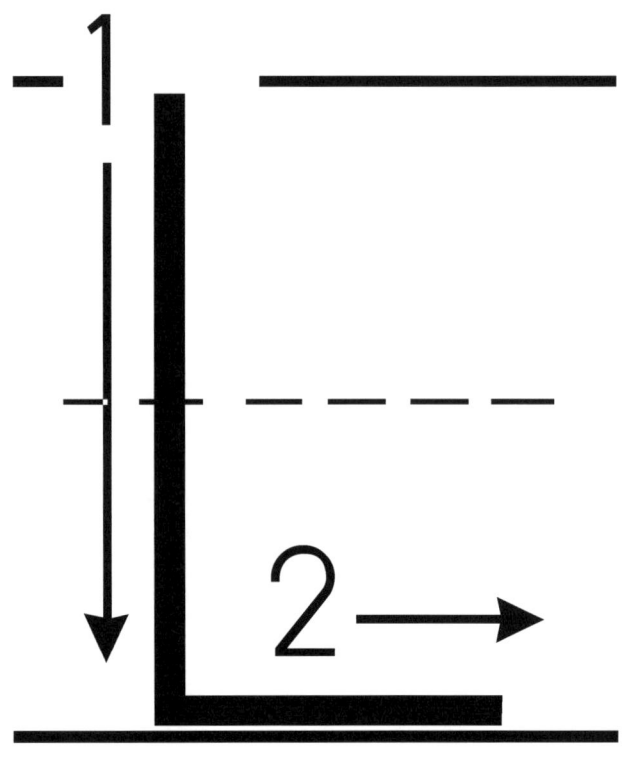

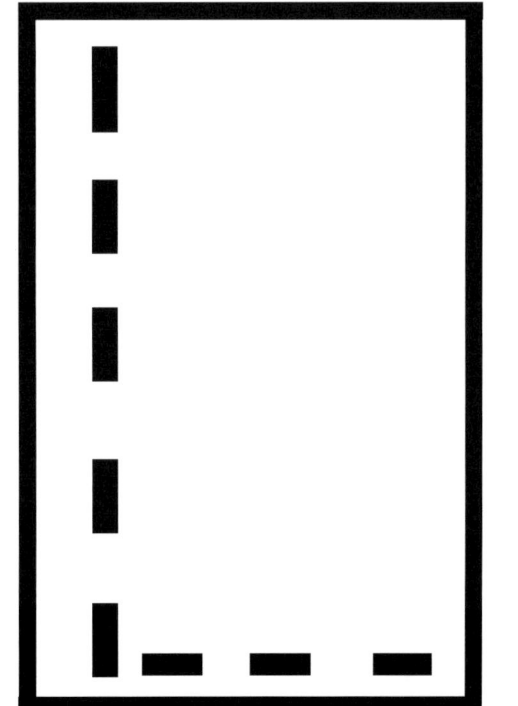

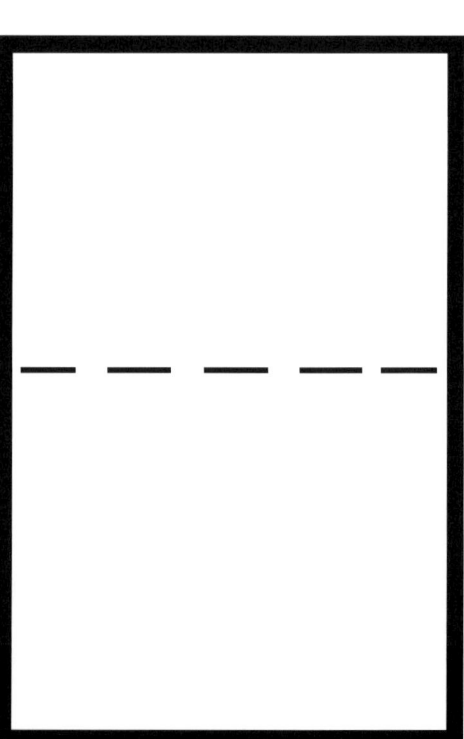

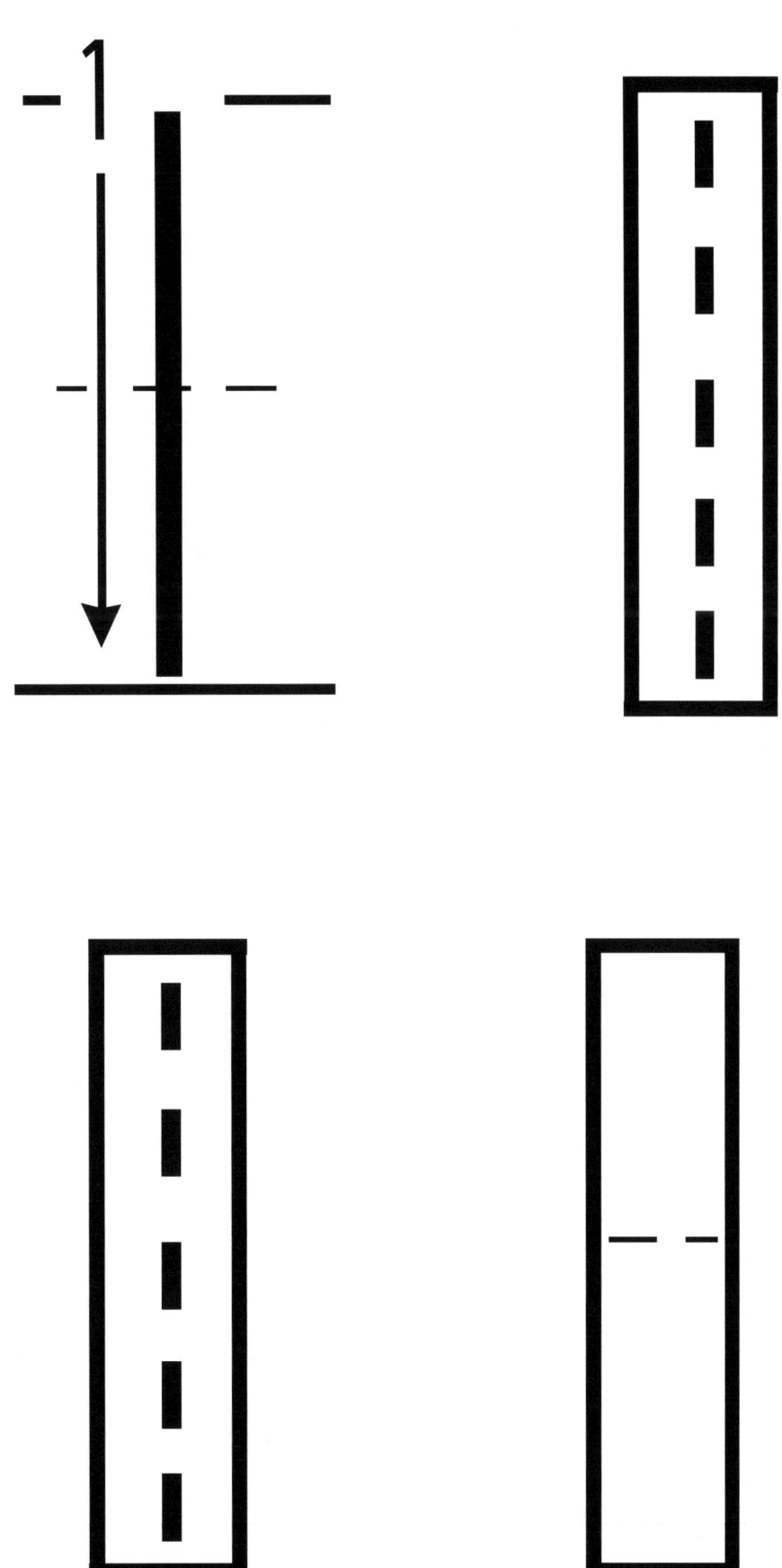

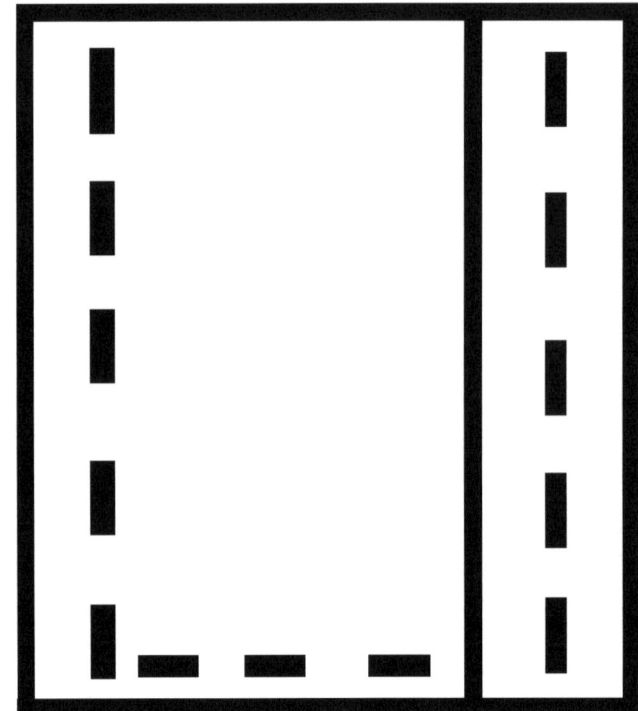

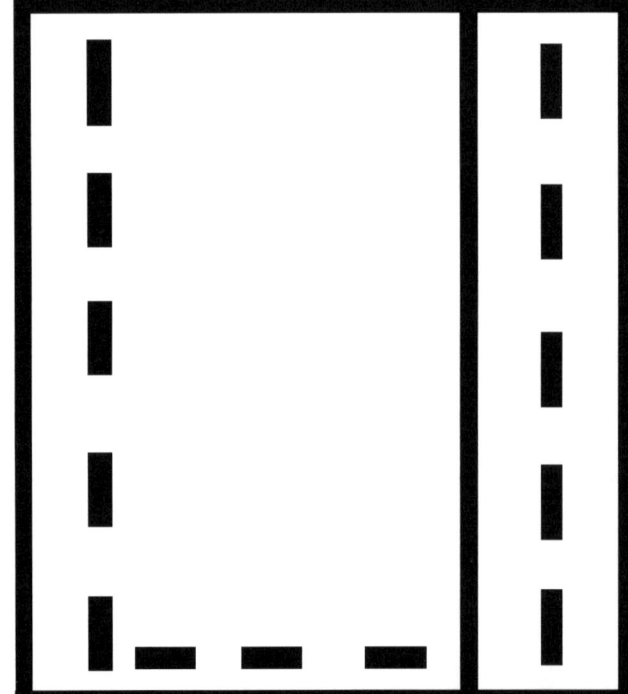

M is for mouse. Color the mouse.

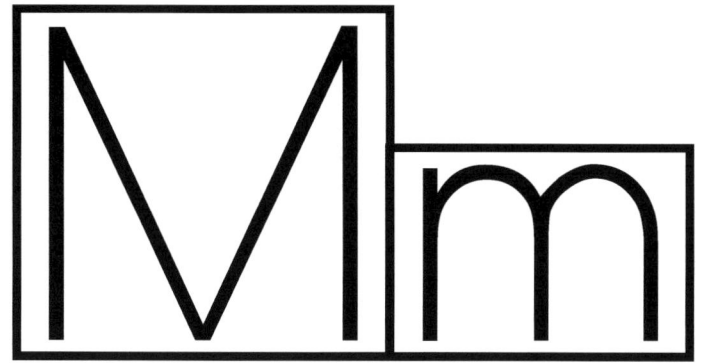

mouse

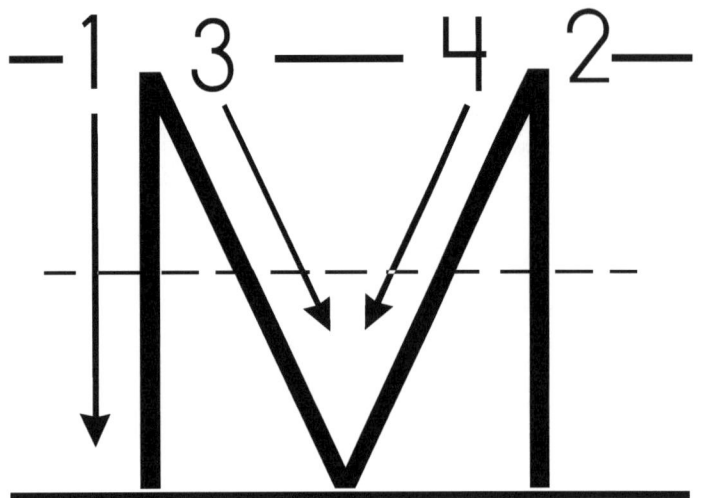

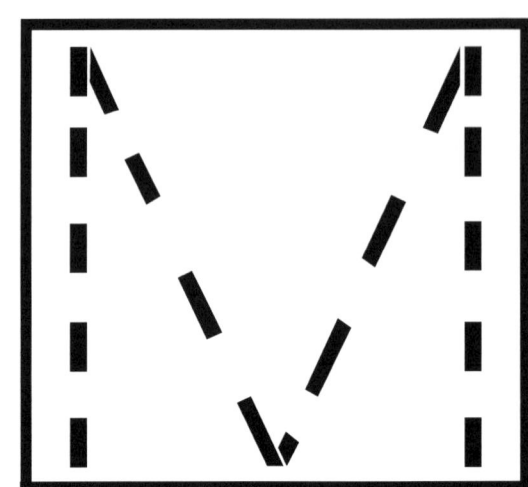

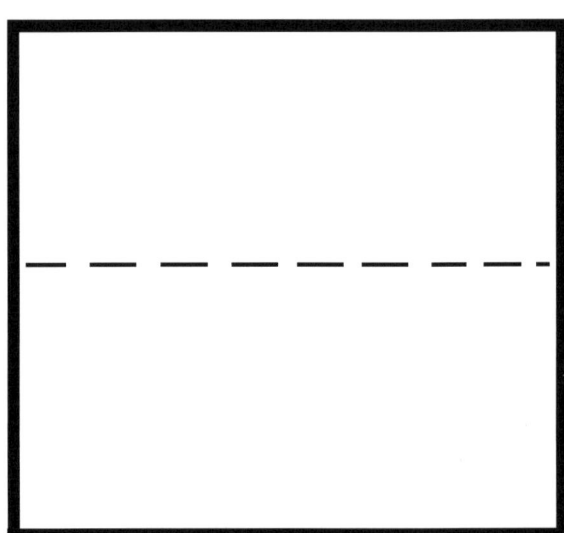

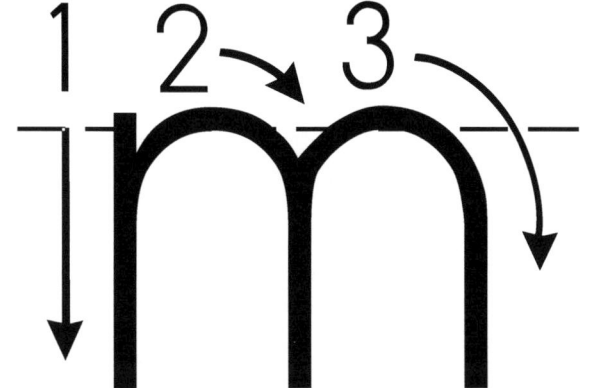

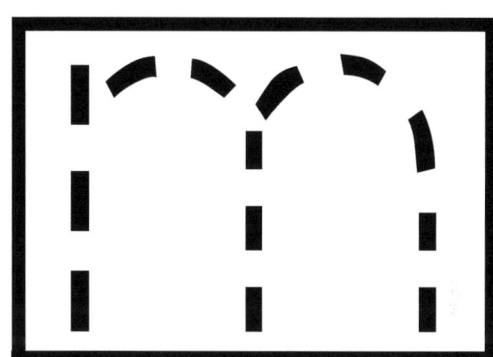

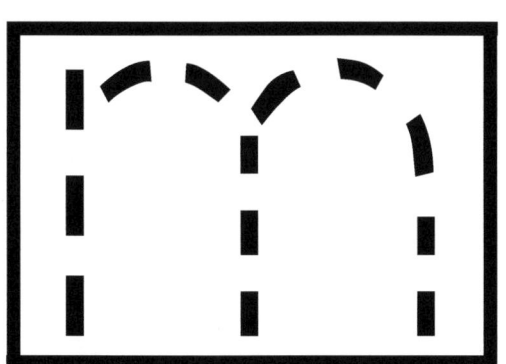

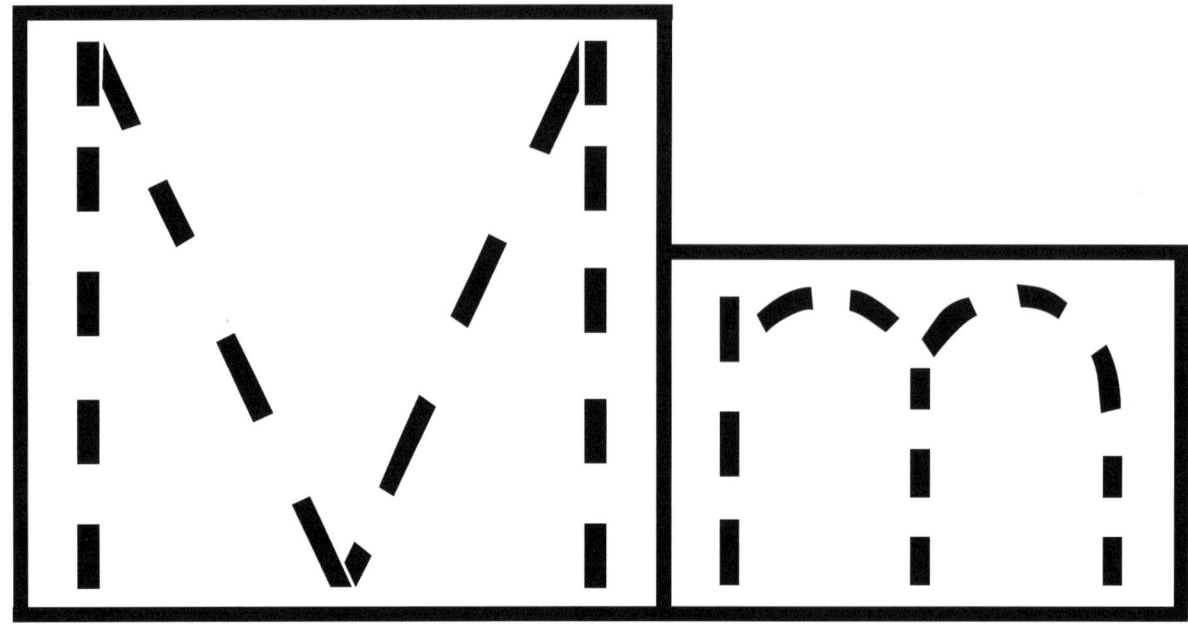

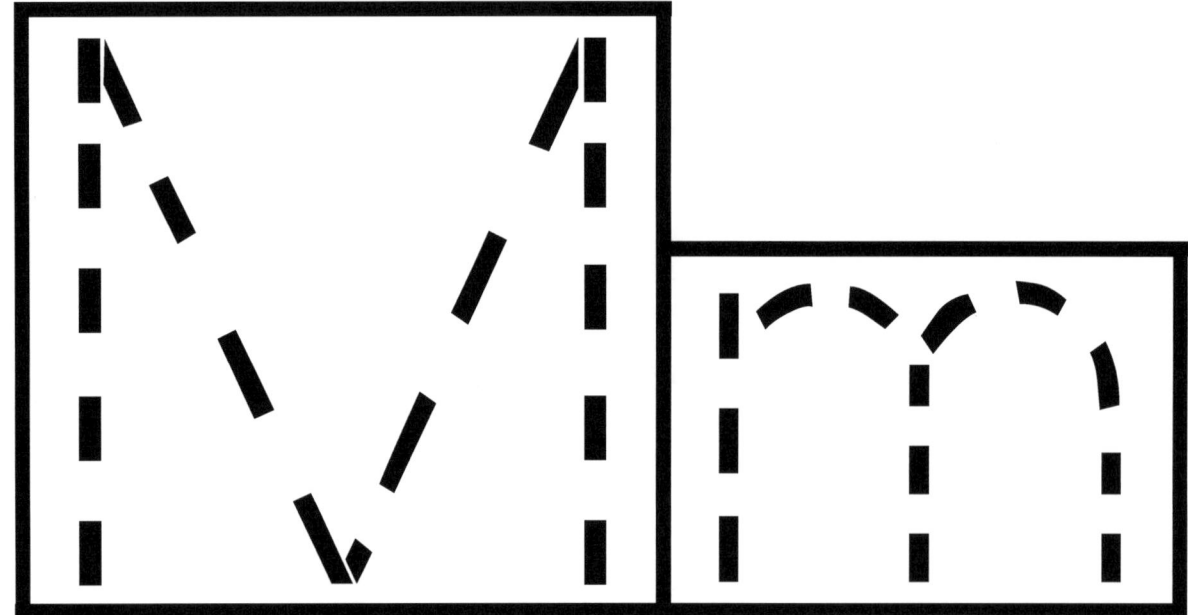

N is for narwhal. Color the narwhal.

Nn

narwhal

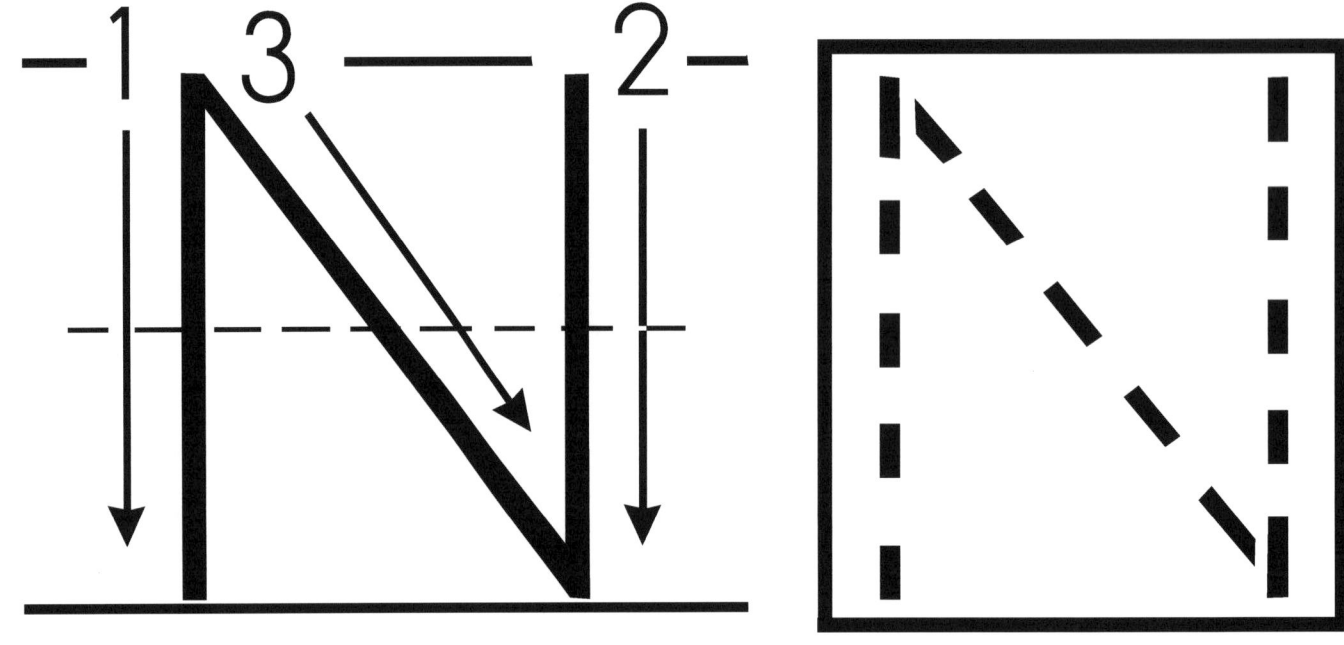

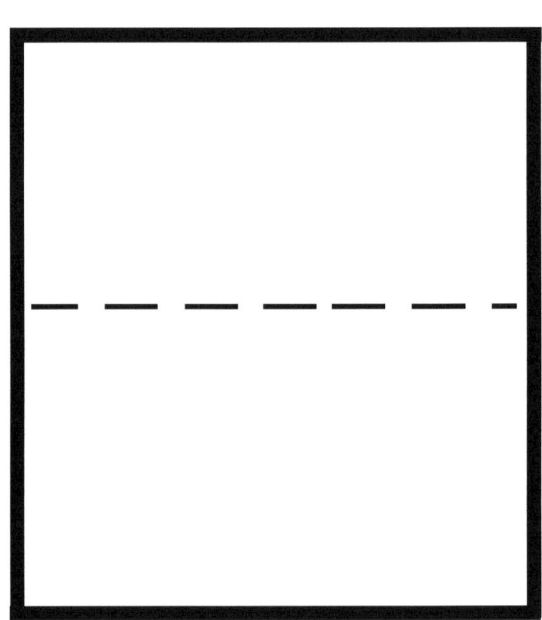

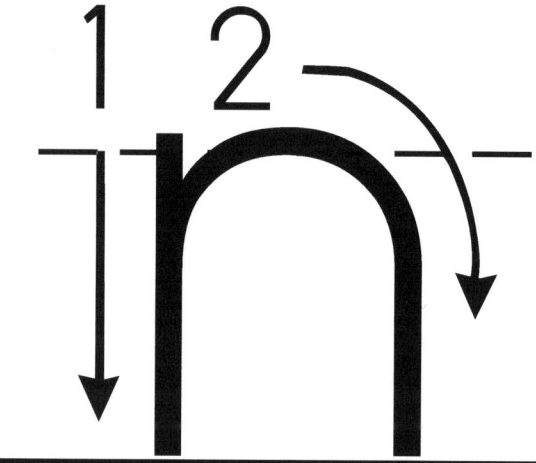

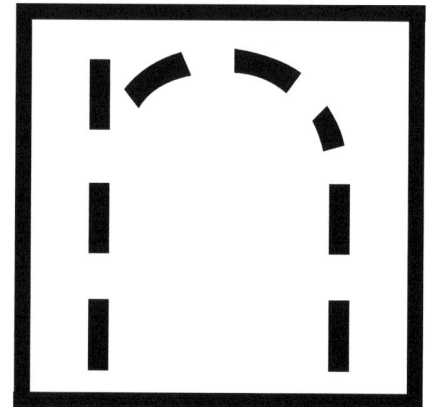

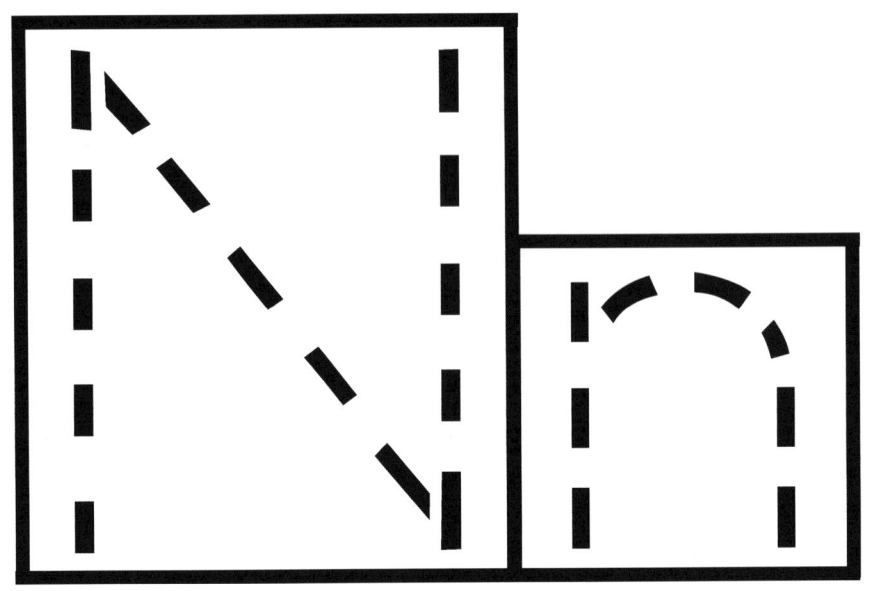

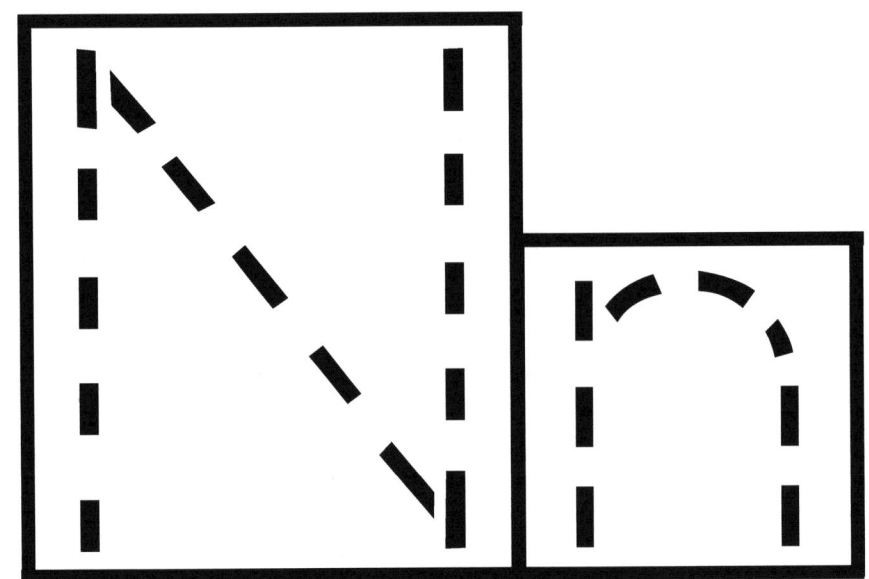

O is for owl. Color the owl.

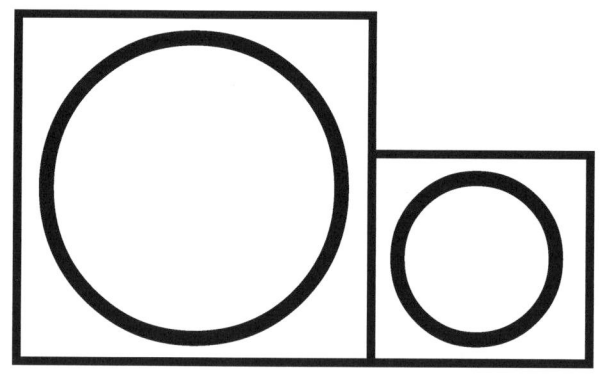

owl

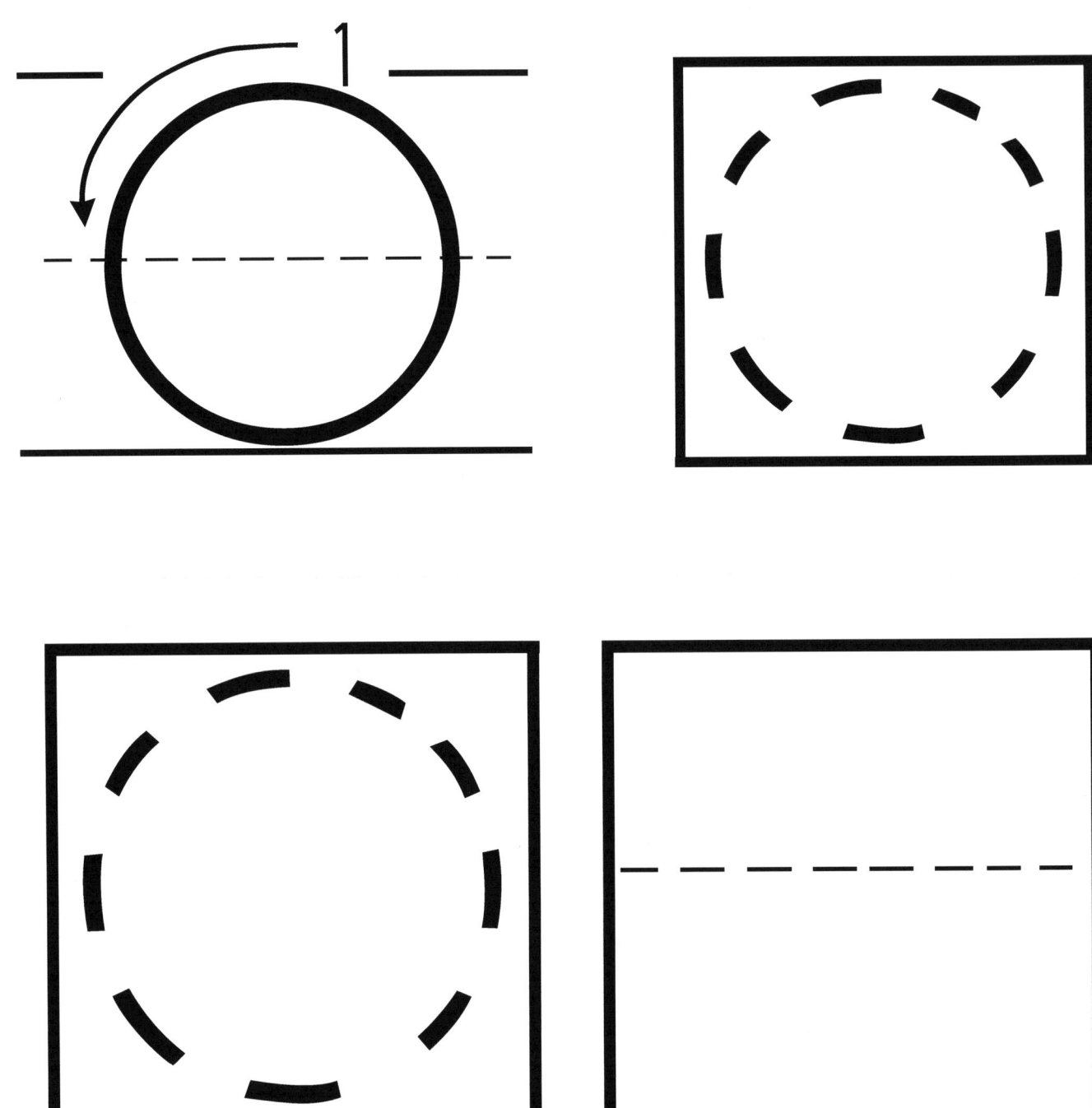

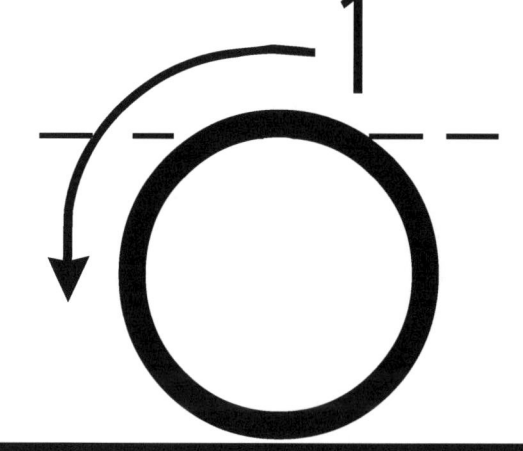

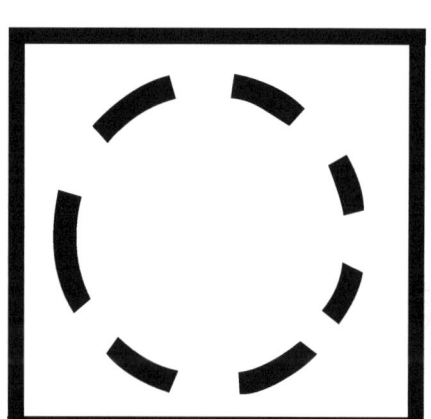

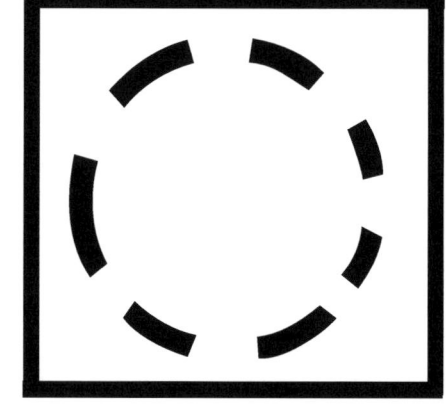

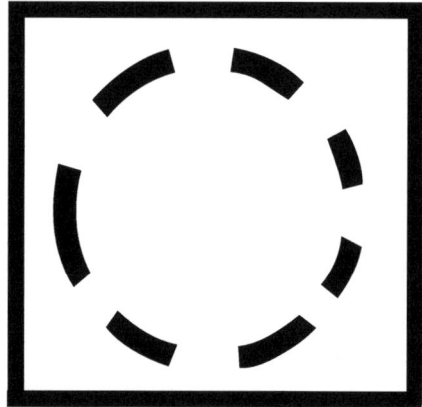

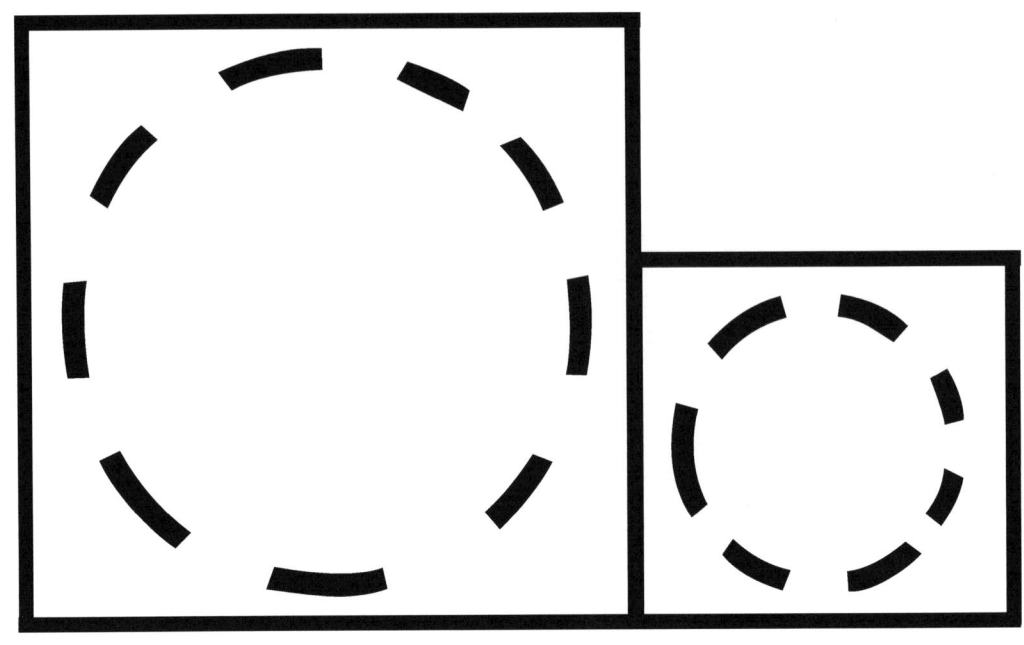

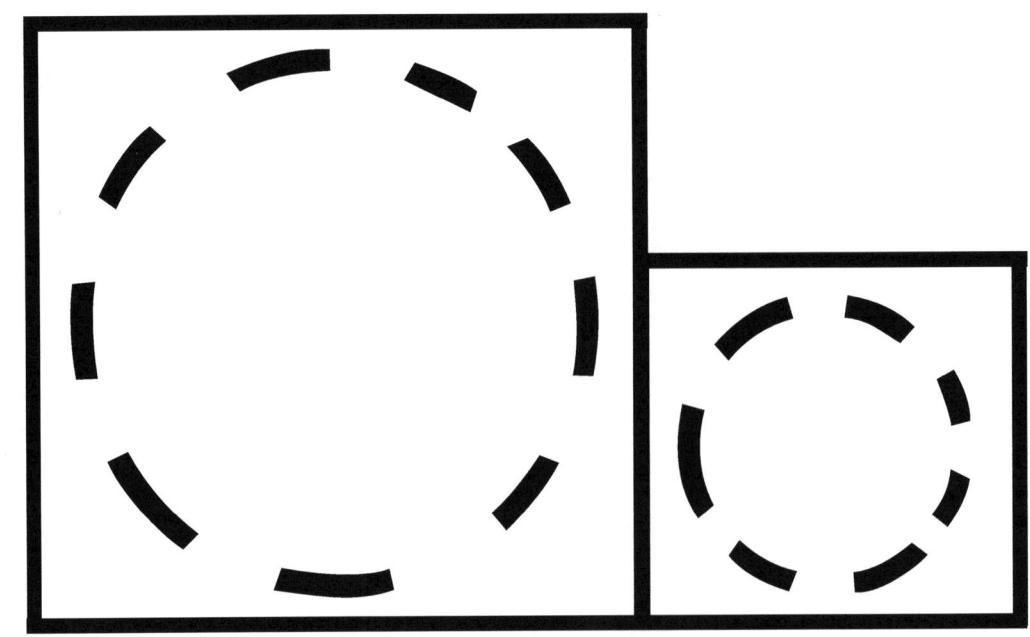

P is for pig. Color the pig.

pig

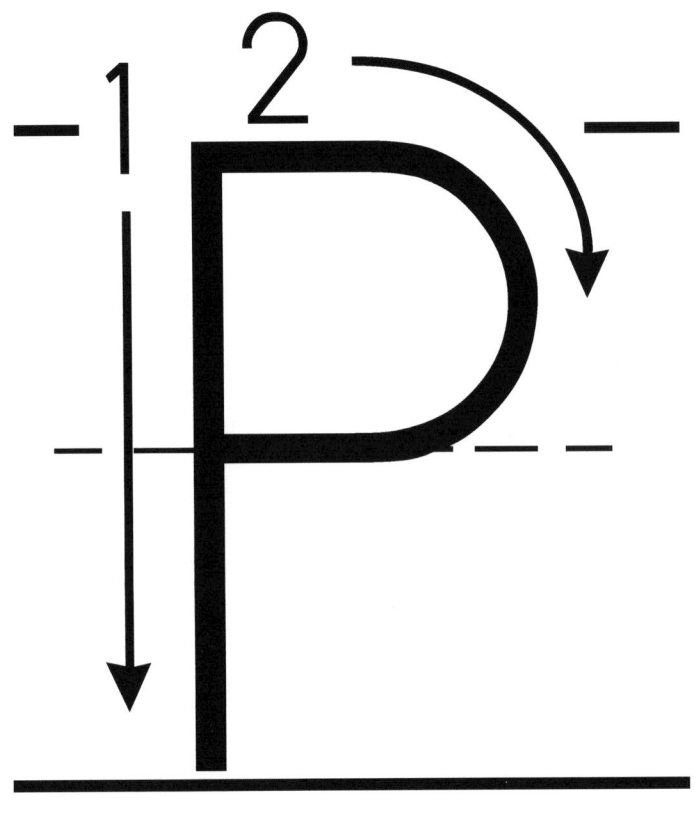

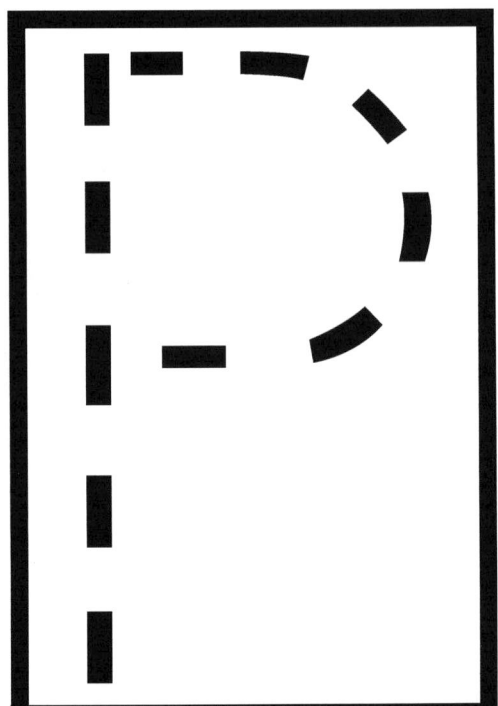

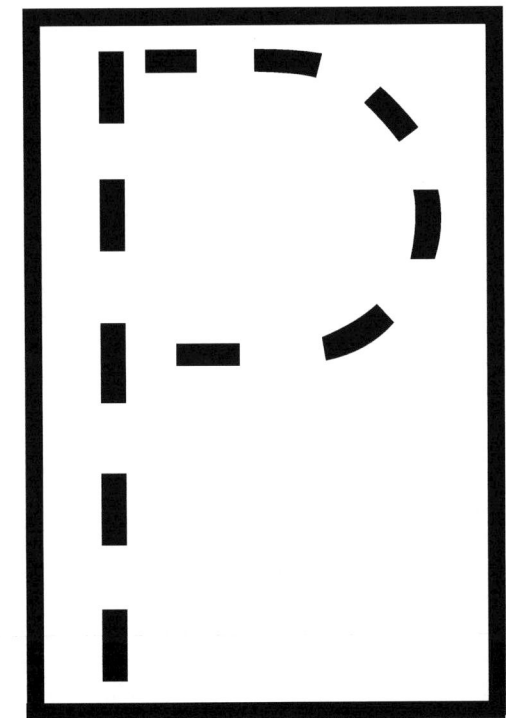

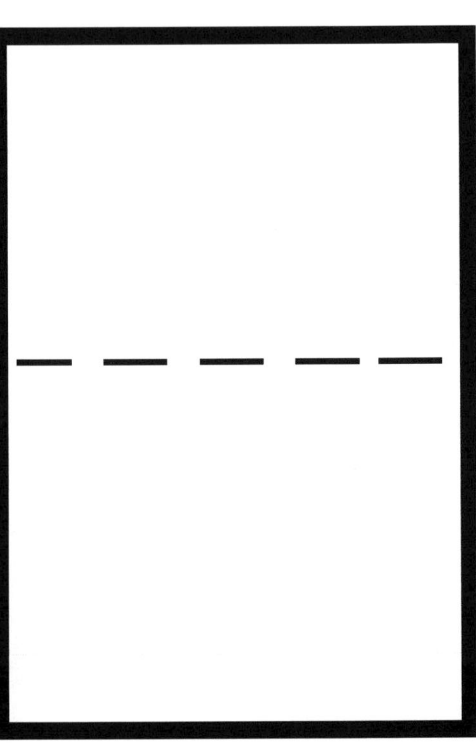

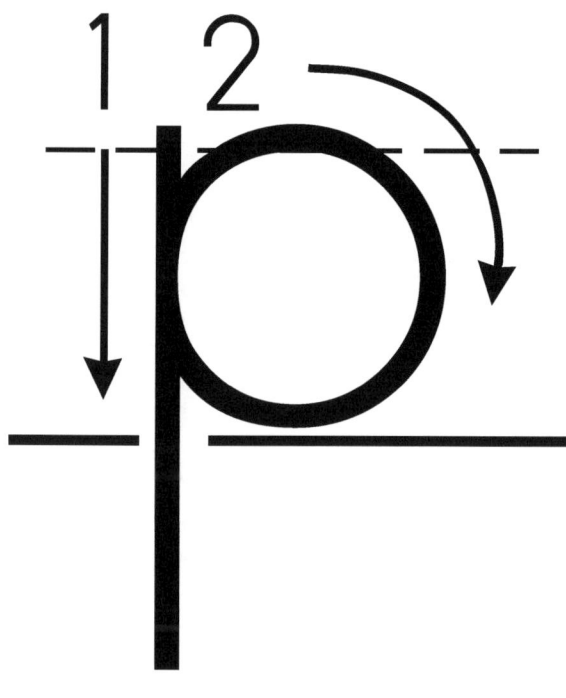

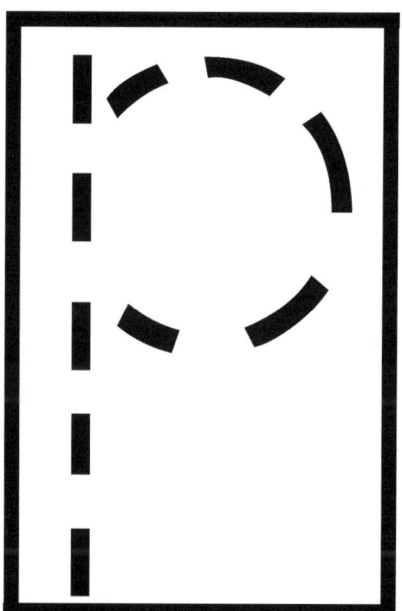

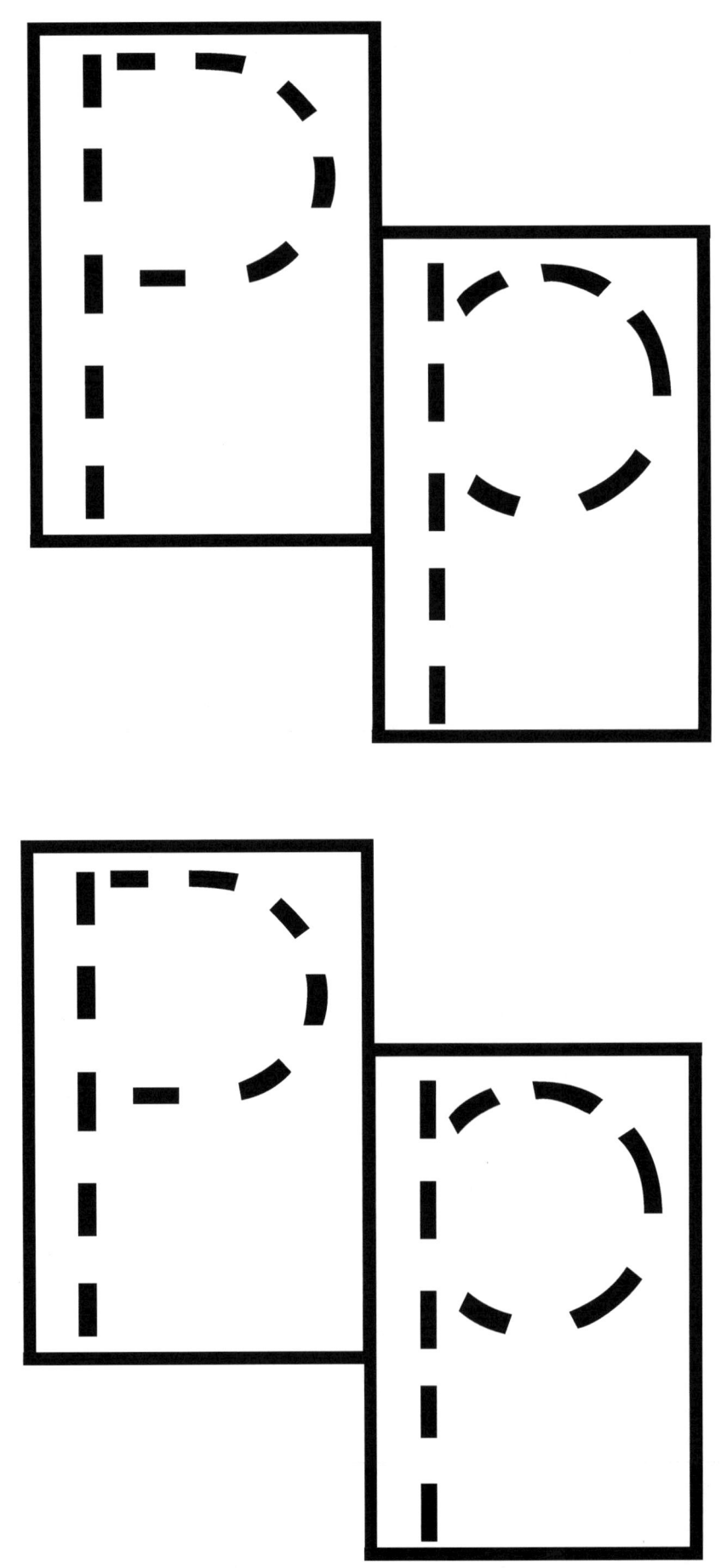

Q is for quetzal. Color the quetzal.

quetzal

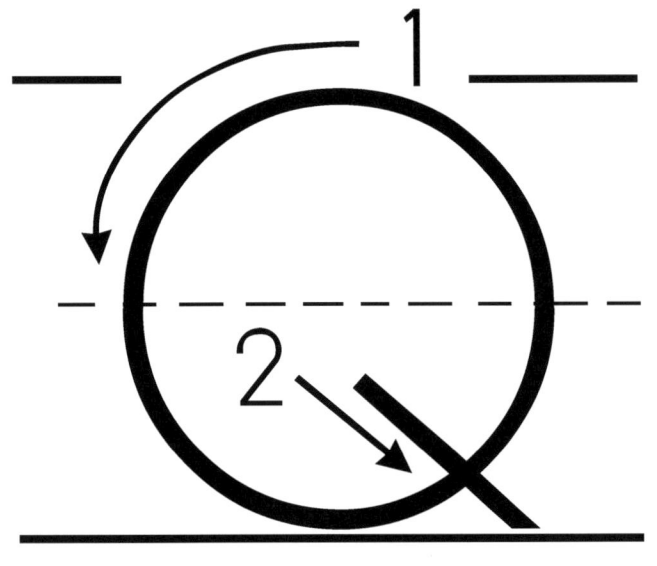
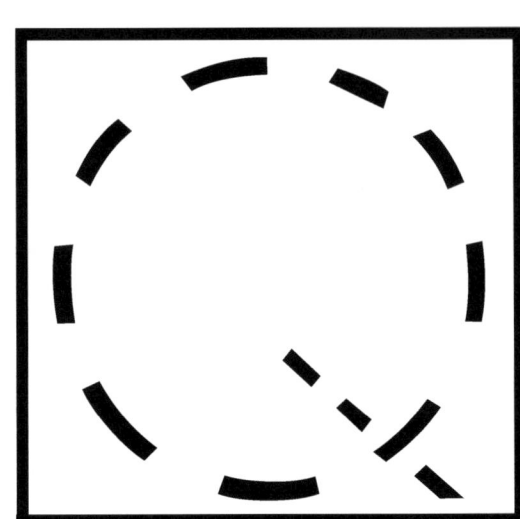
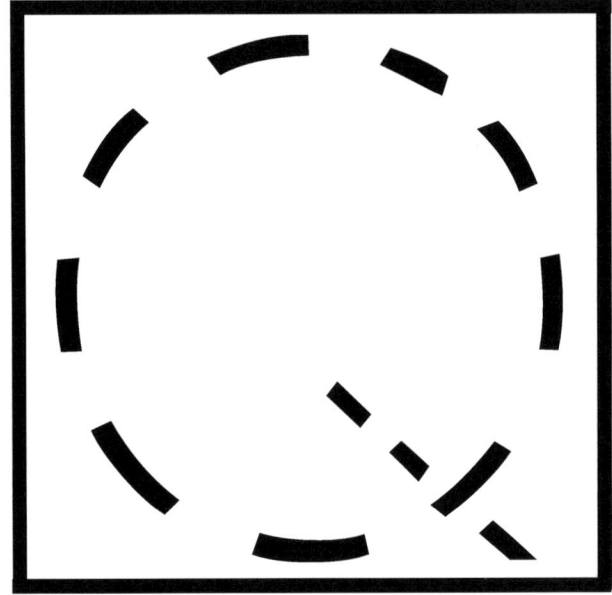
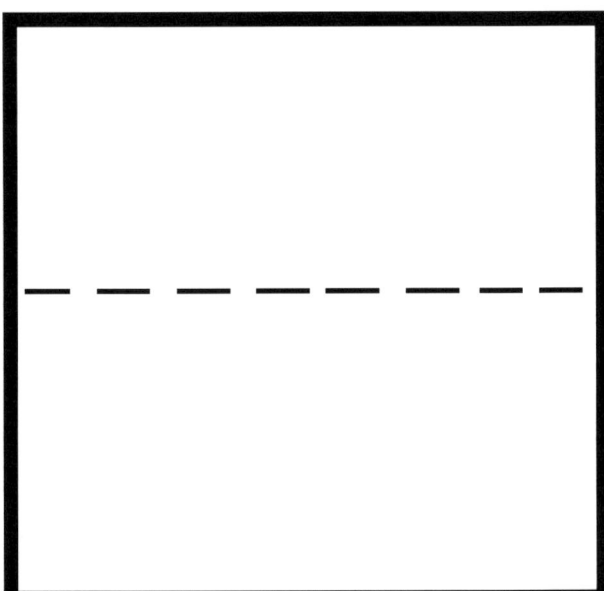

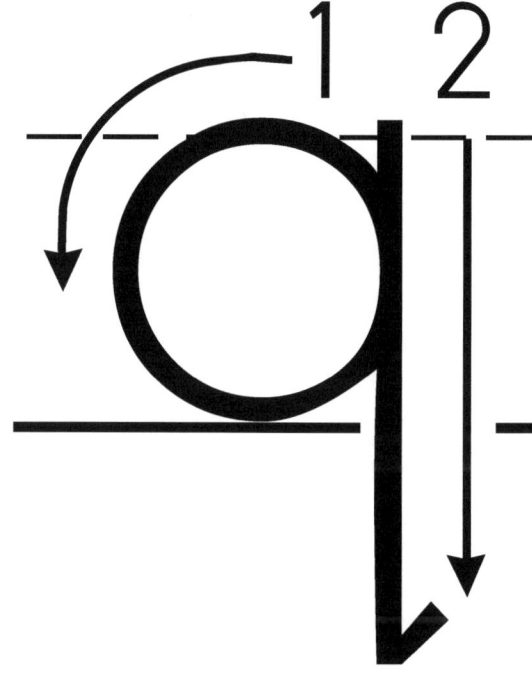

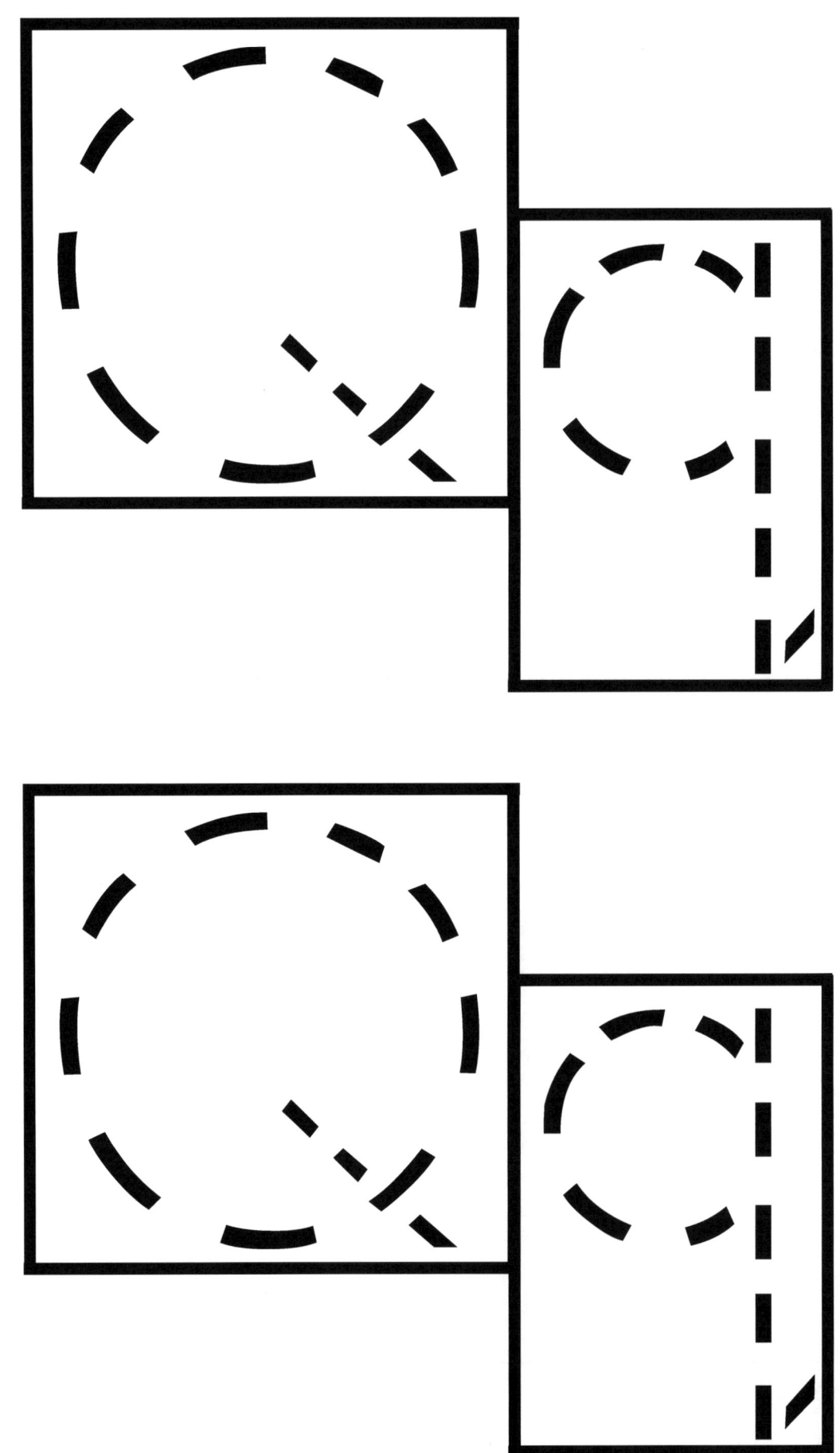

R is for raccoon. Color the raccoon.

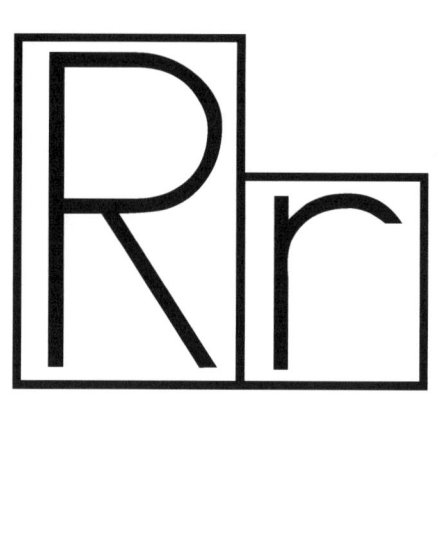

raccoon

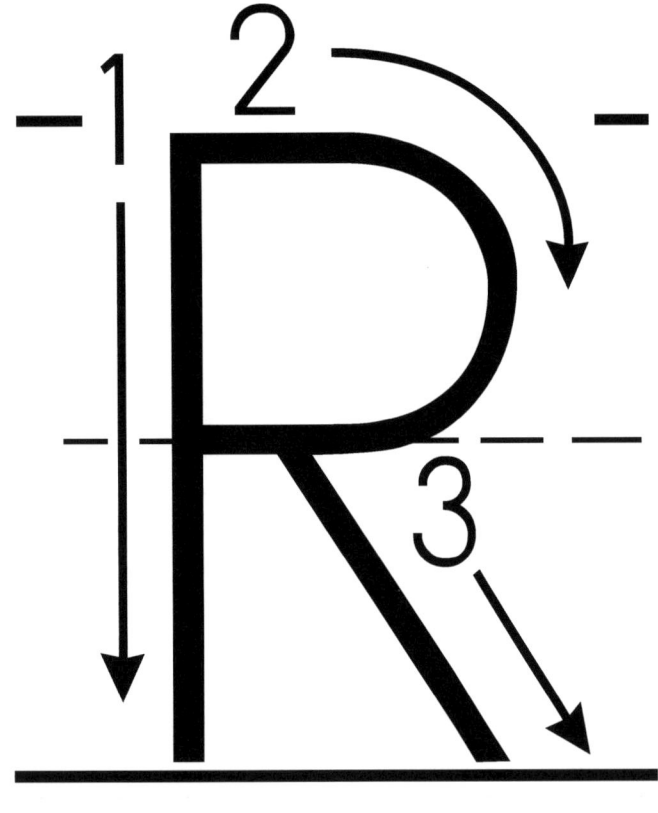

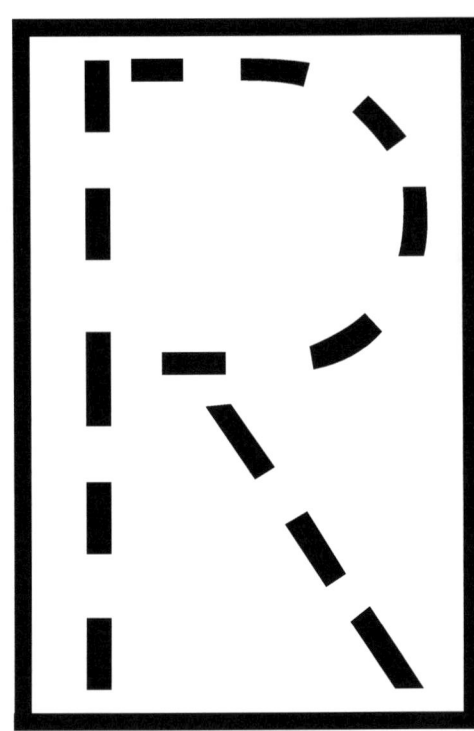

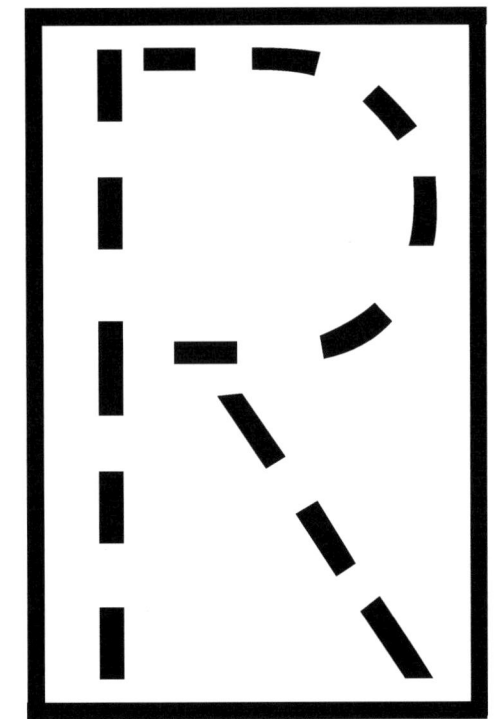

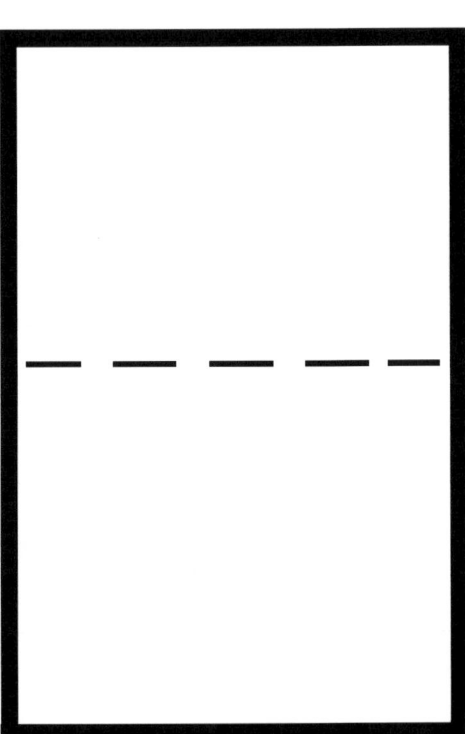

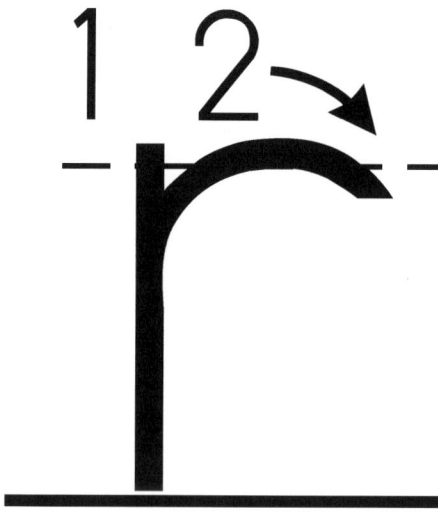

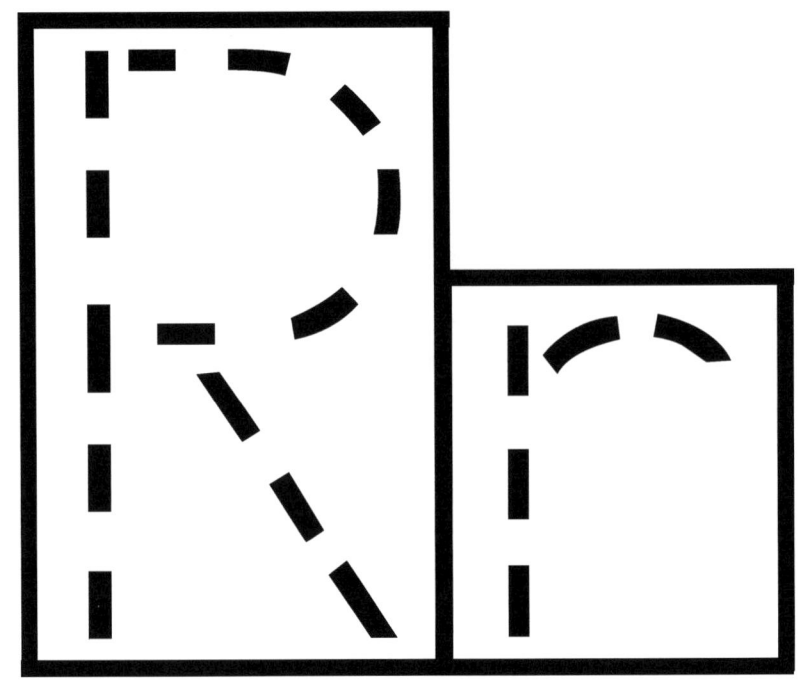

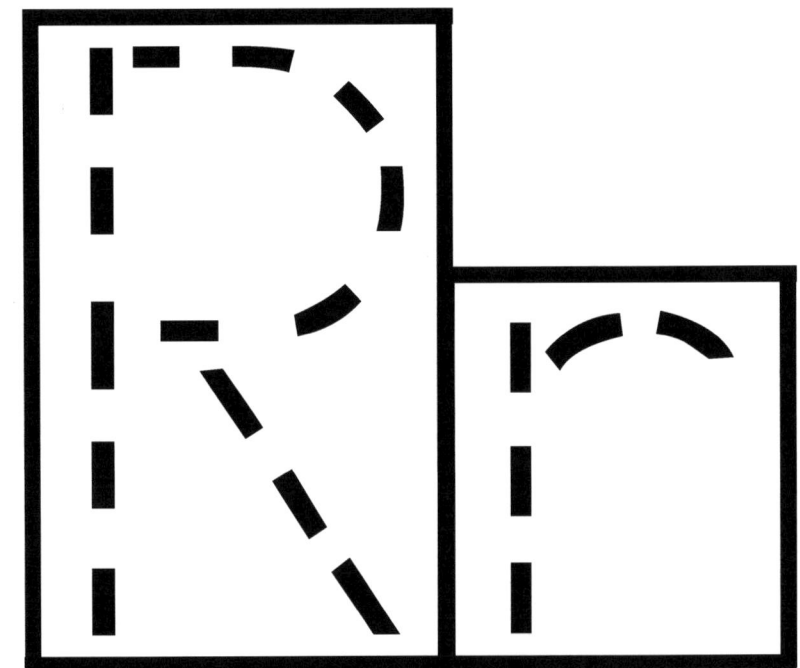

S is for squirrel. Color the squirrel.

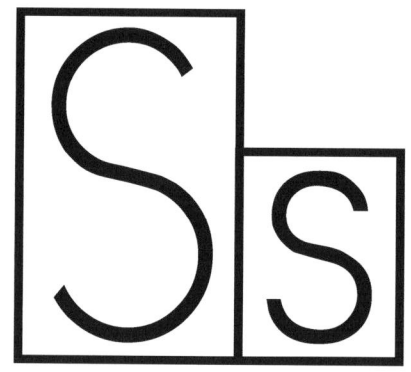

squirrel

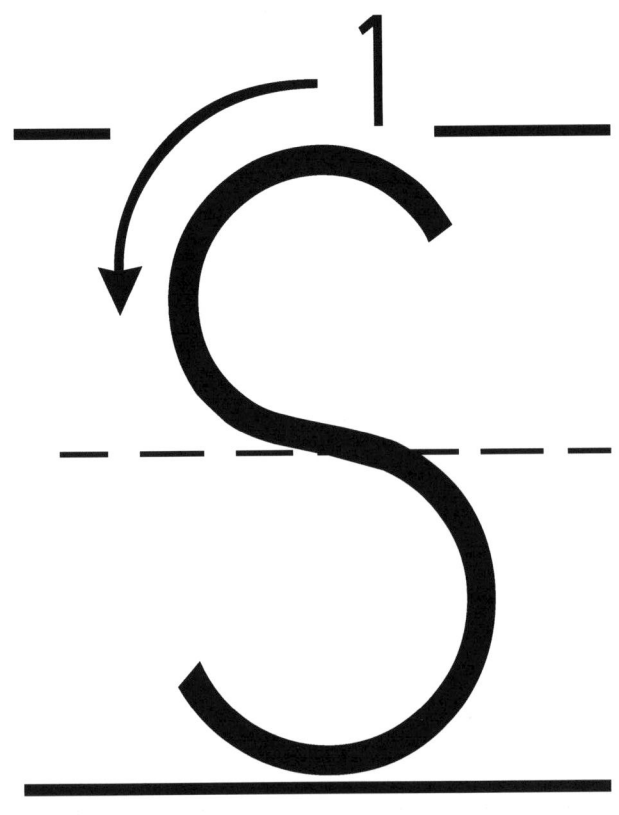

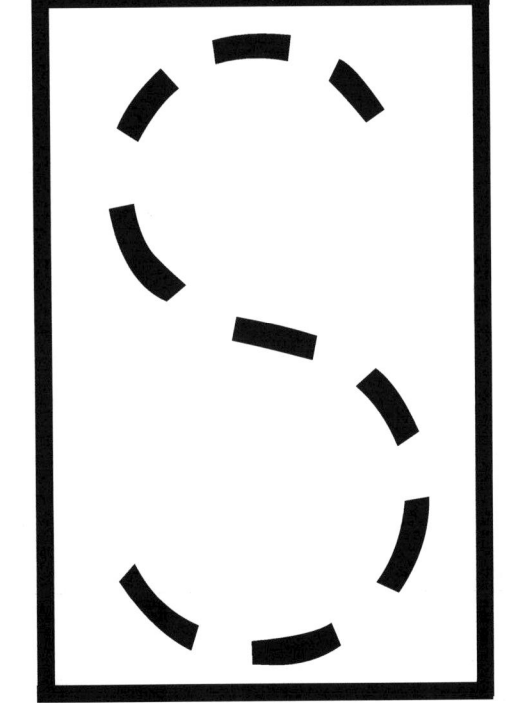

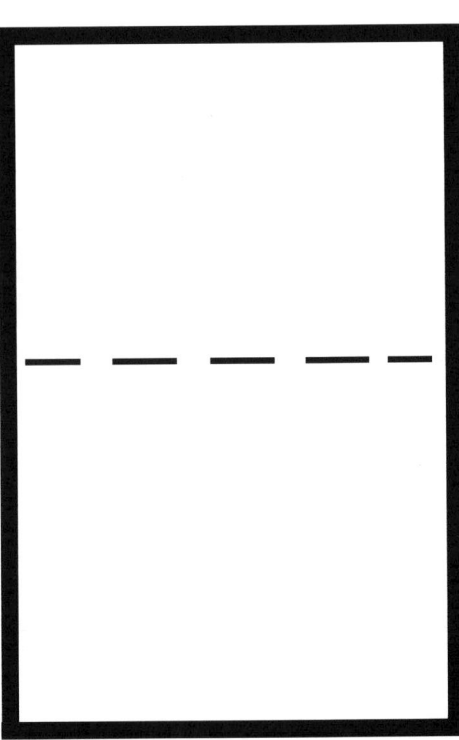

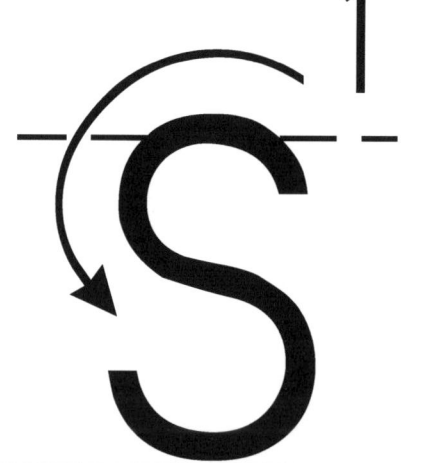

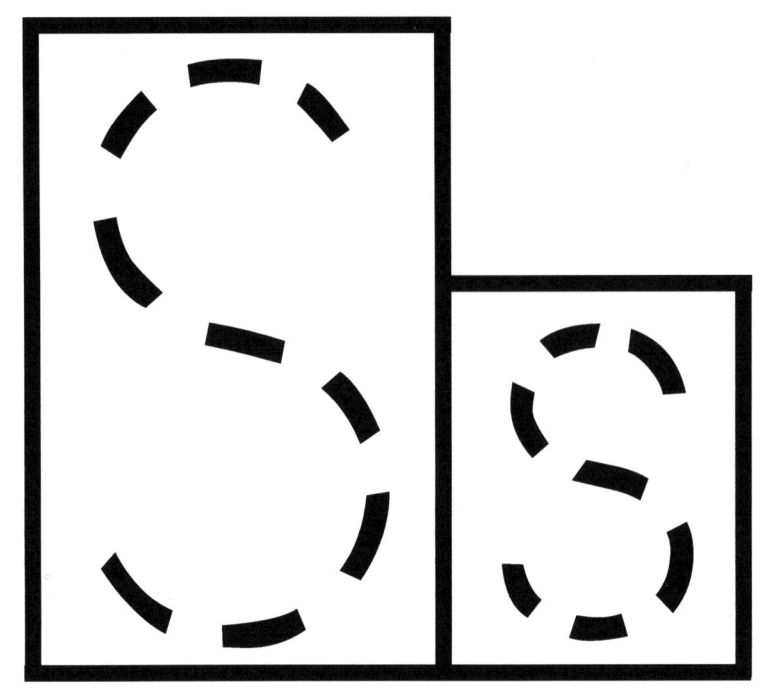

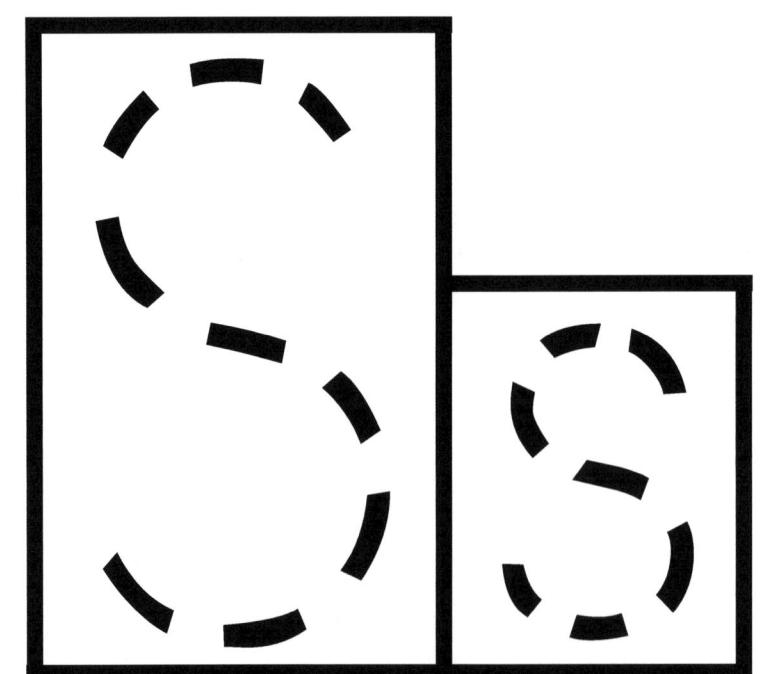

T is for toucan. Color the toucan.

toucan

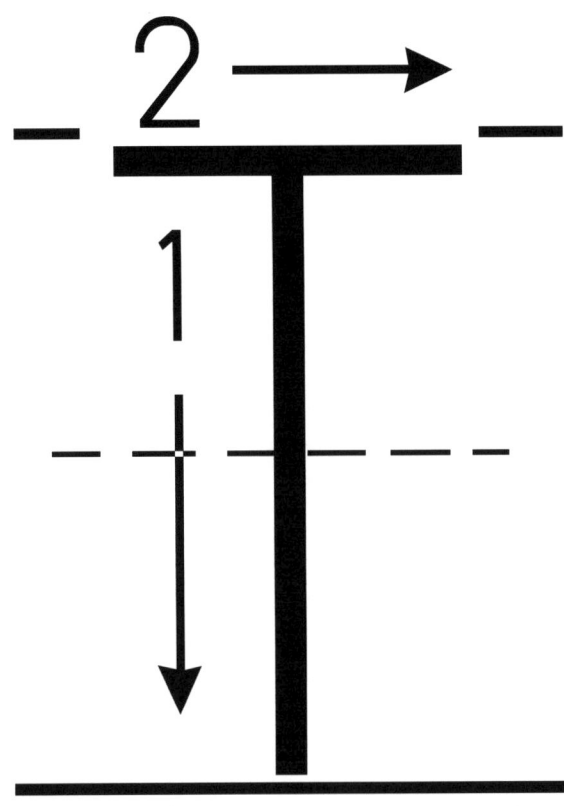

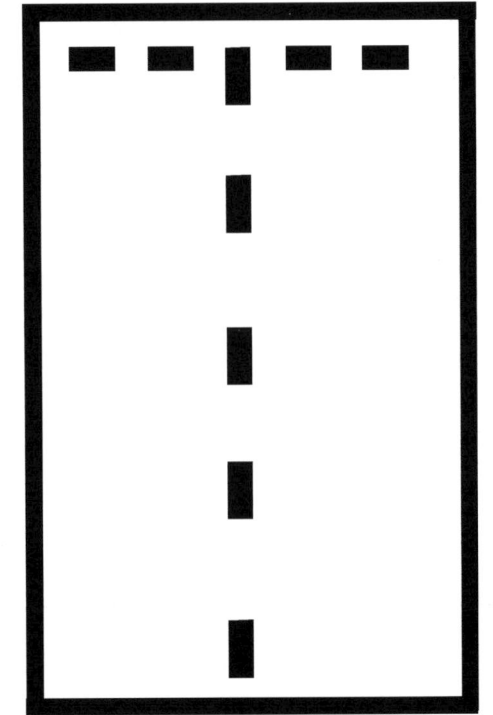

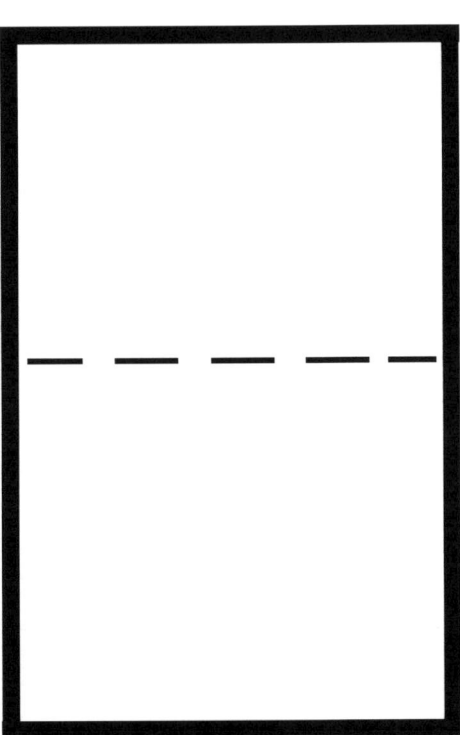

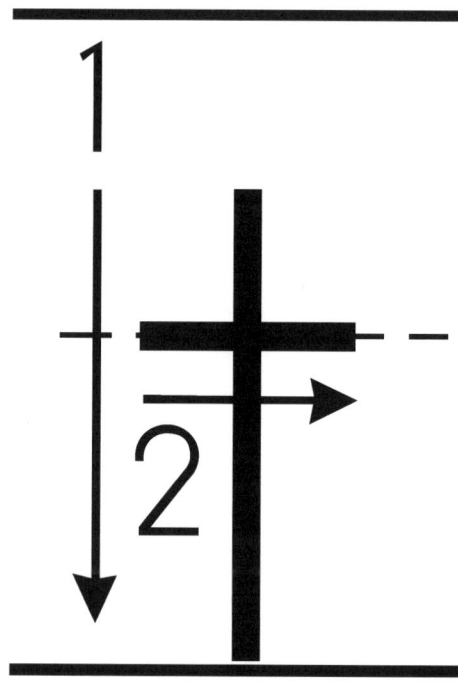

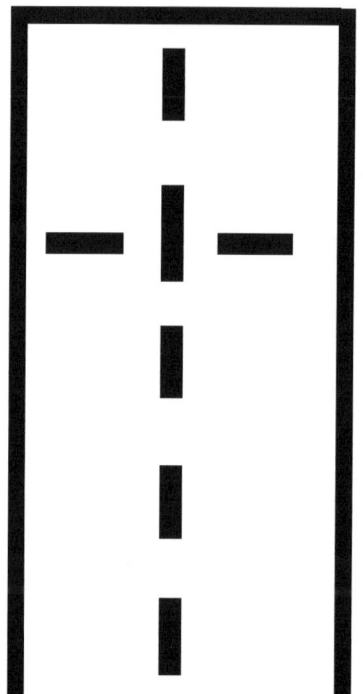

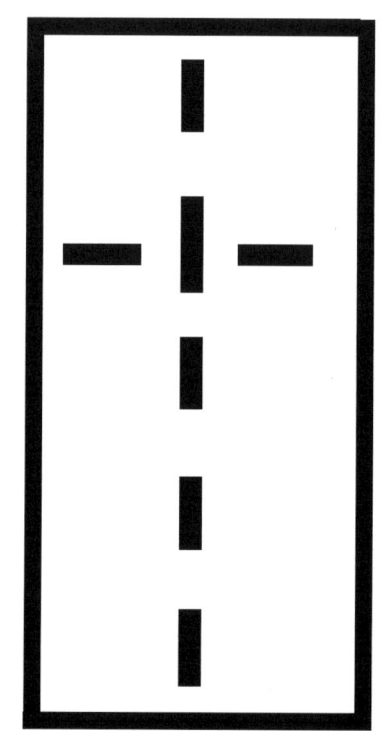

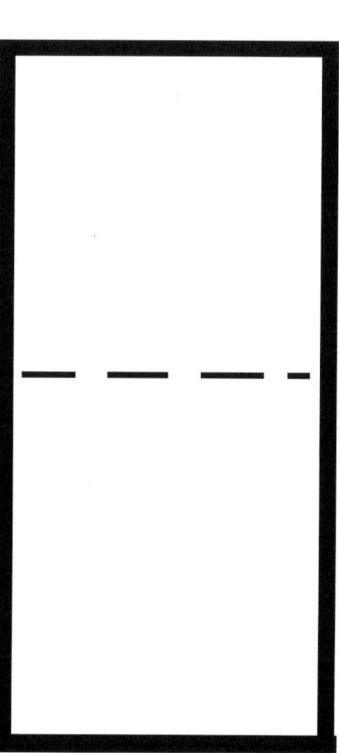

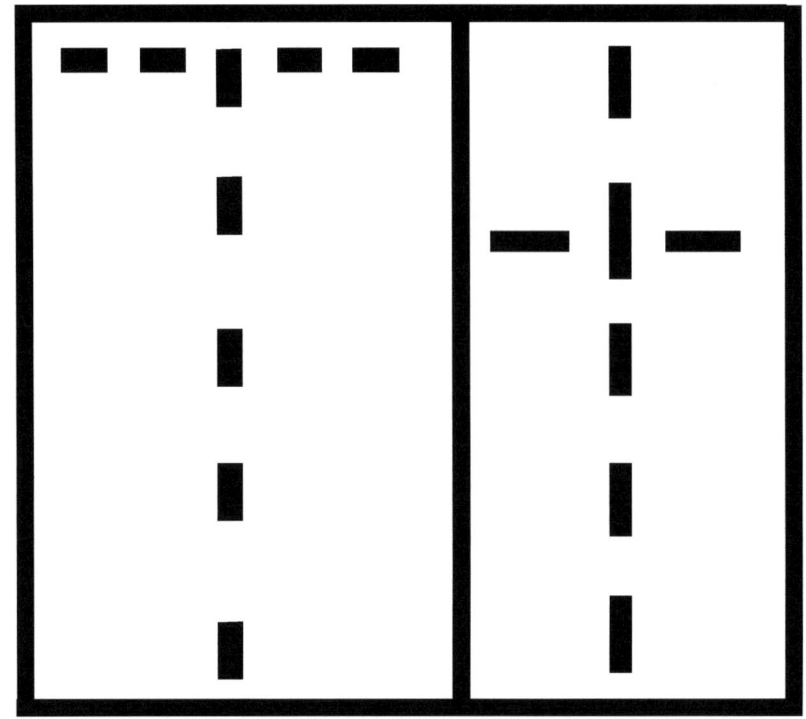

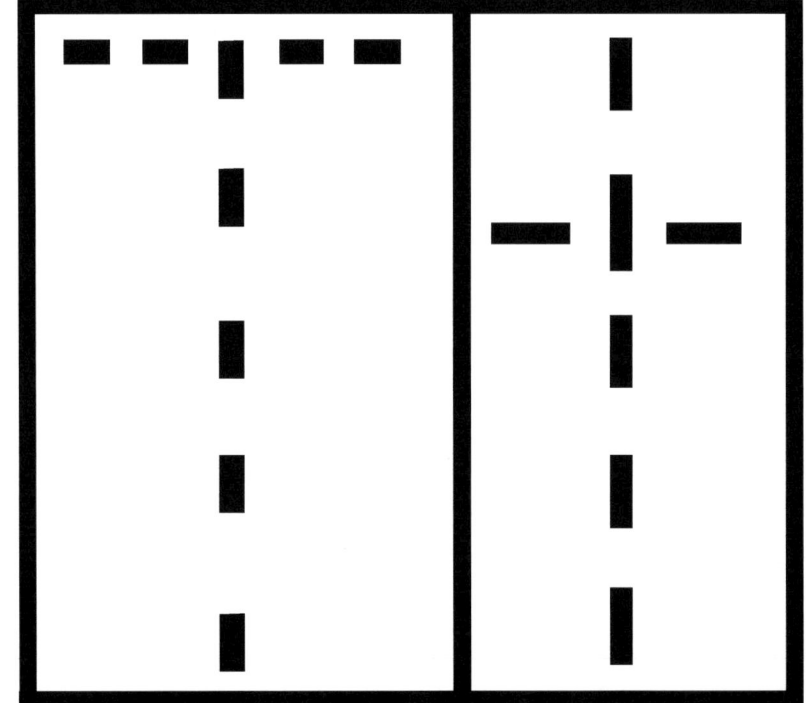

U is for unicorn. Color the unicorn.

unicorn

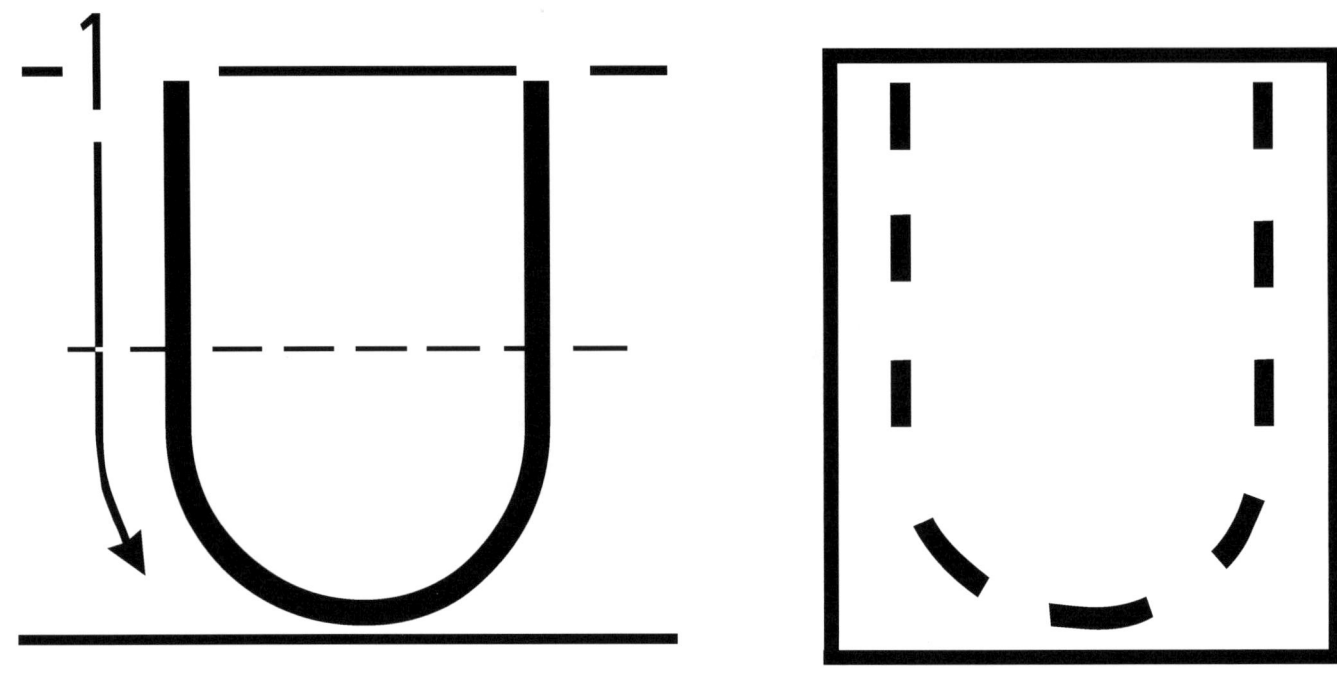

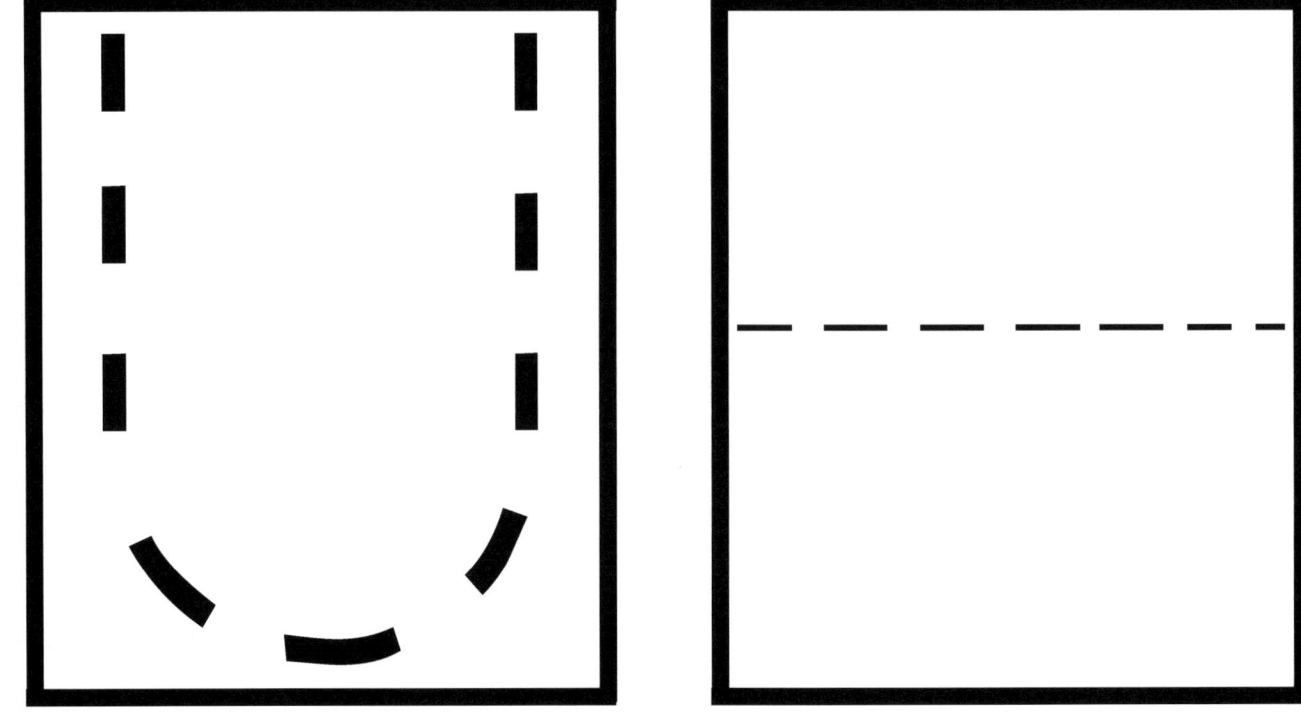

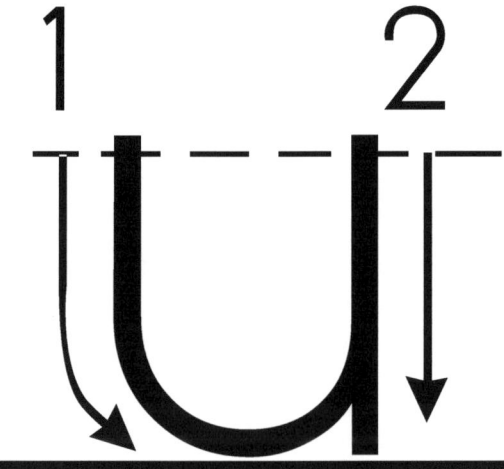

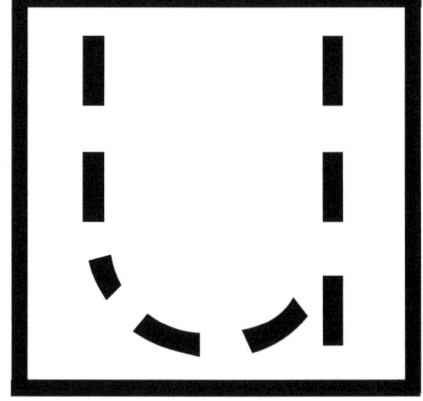

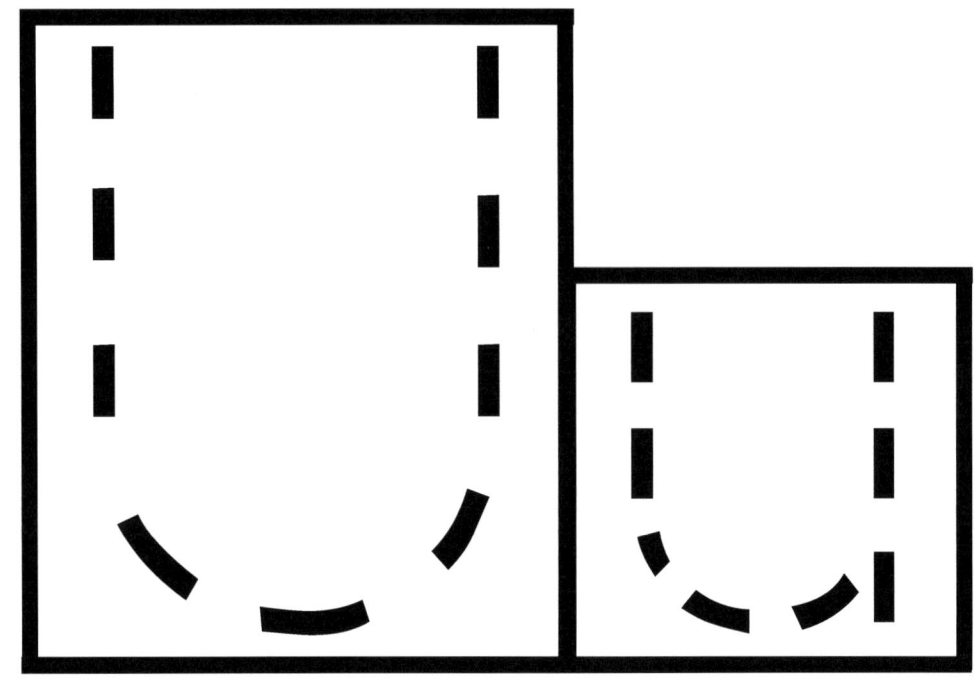

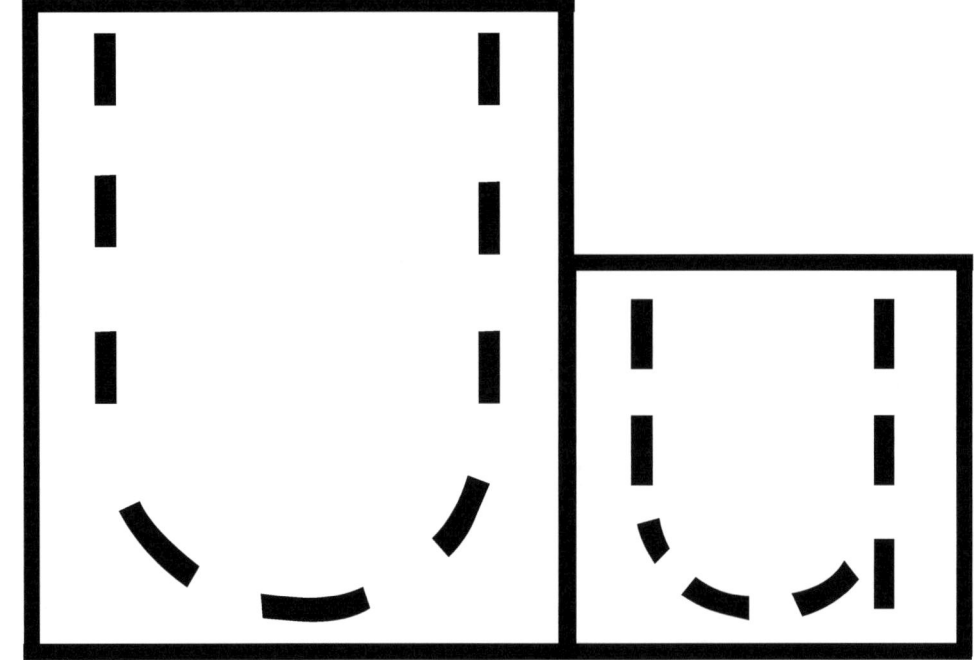

V is for vulture. Color the vulture.

vulture

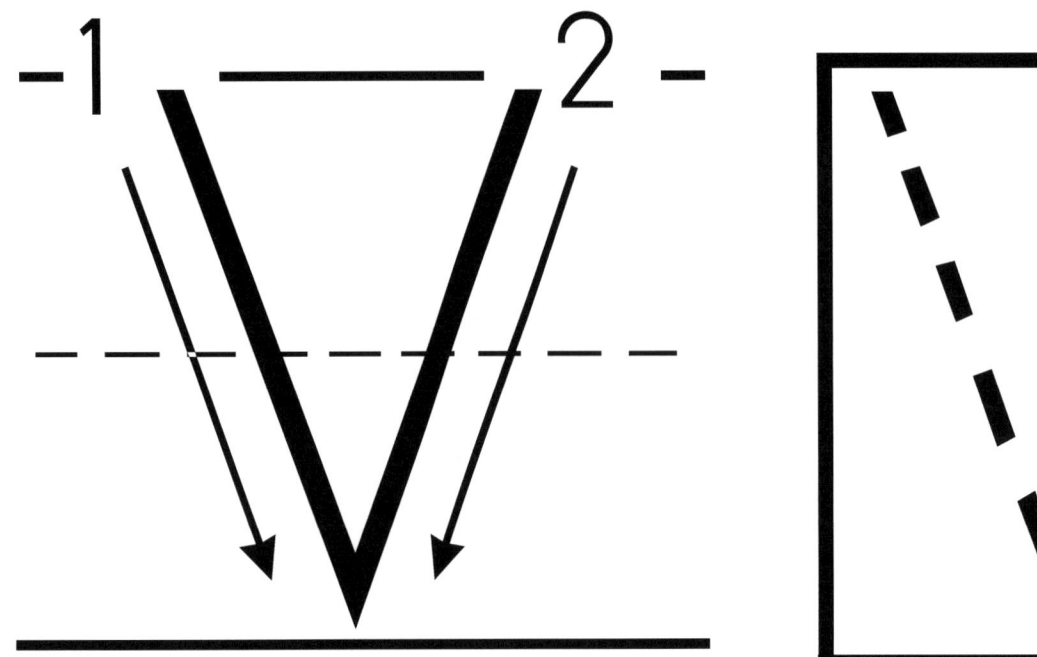

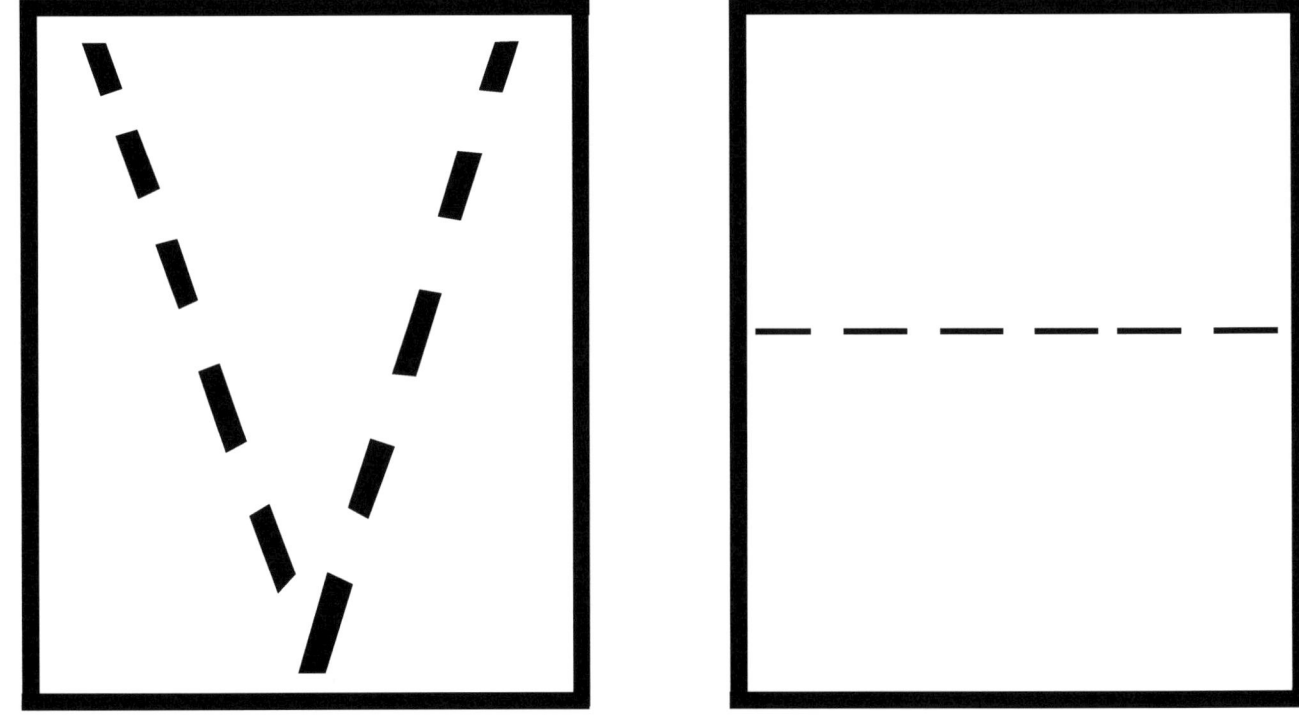

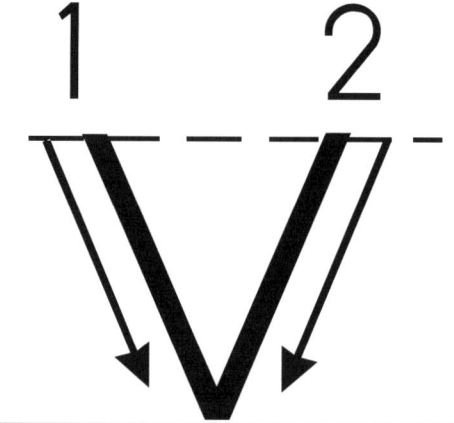

1   2

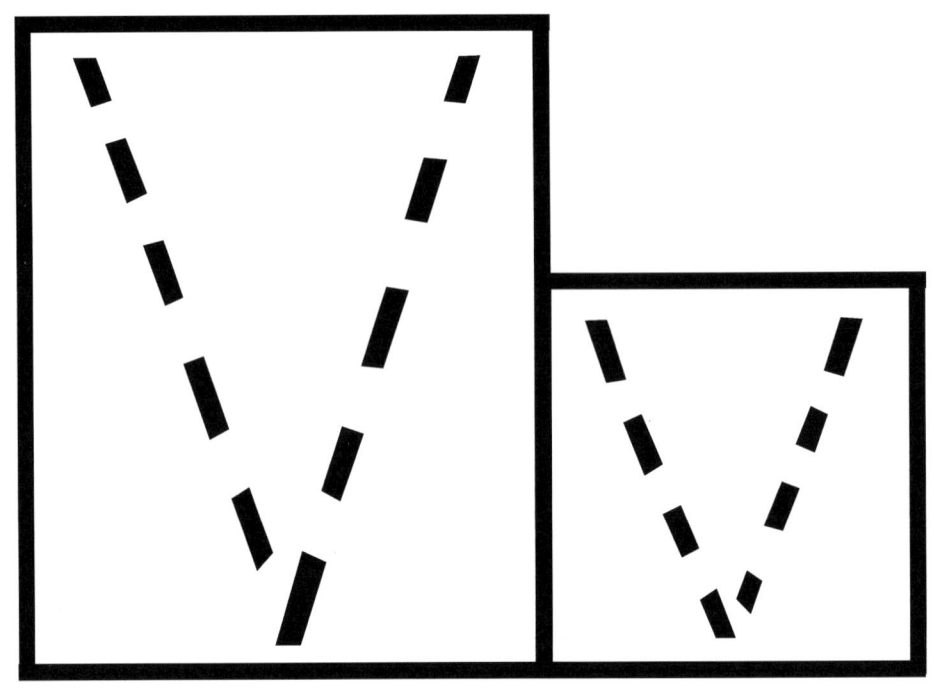

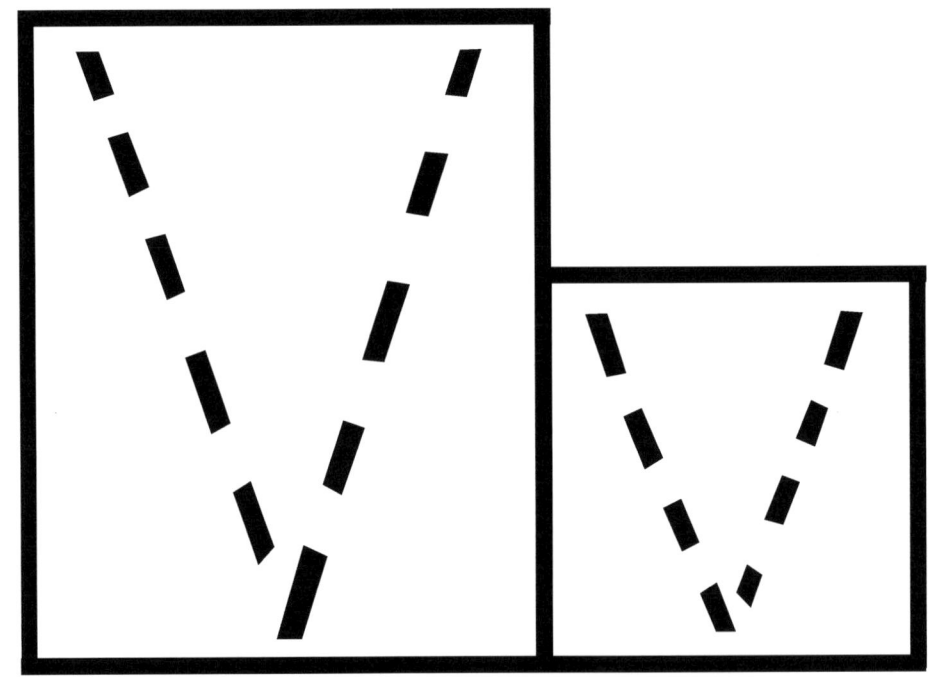

W is for walrus. Color the walrus.

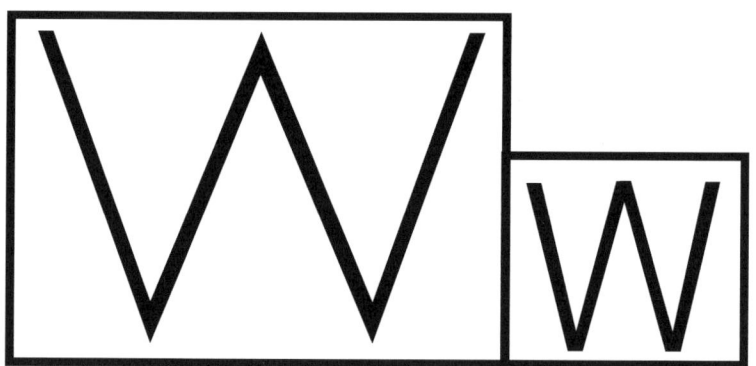

walrus

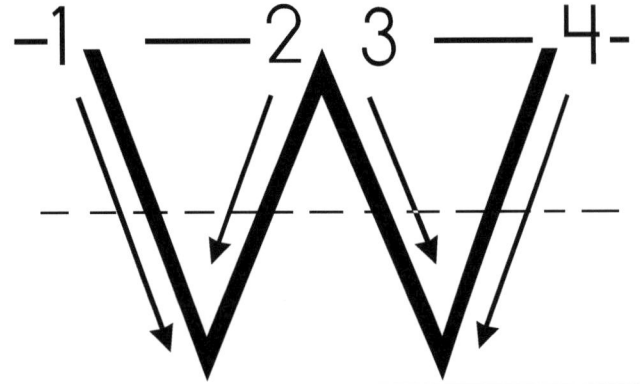

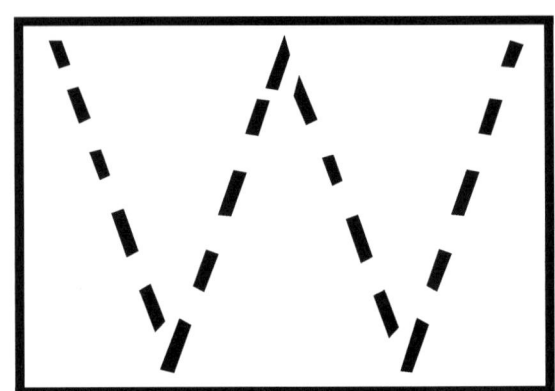

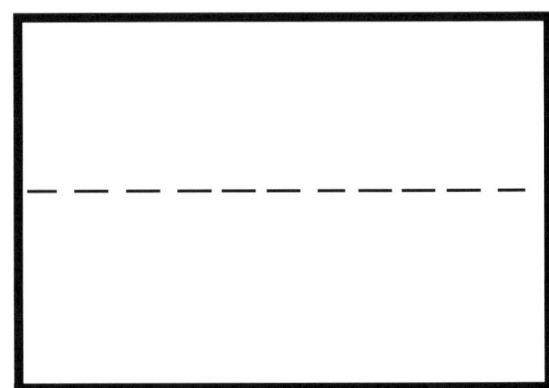

1 2 3 4

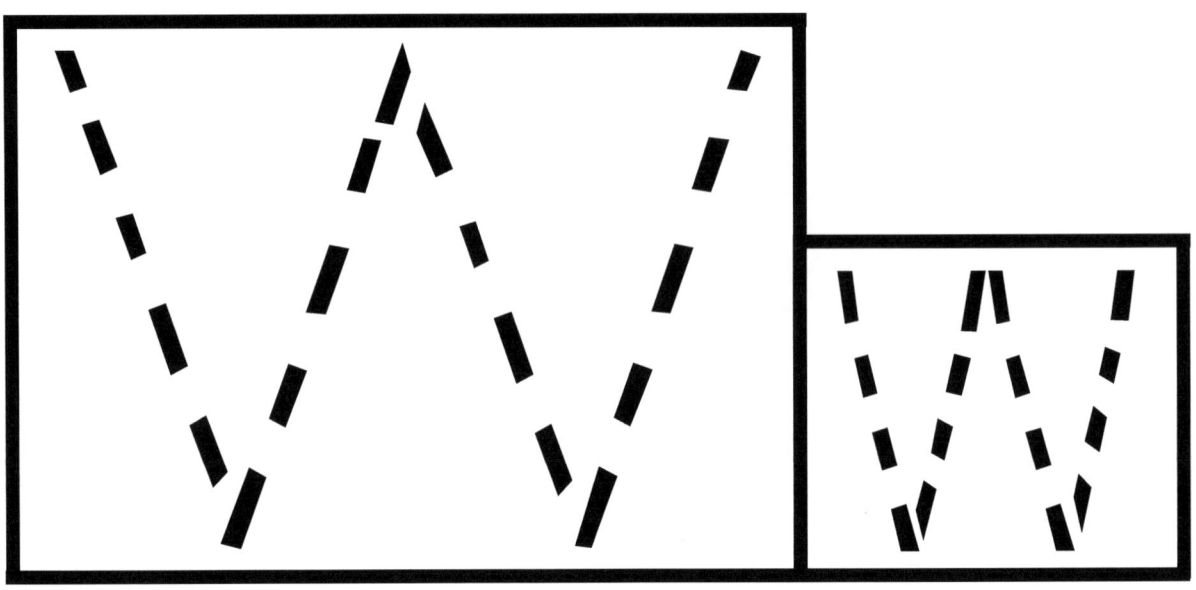

X is for X-ray fish. Color the X-ray fish.

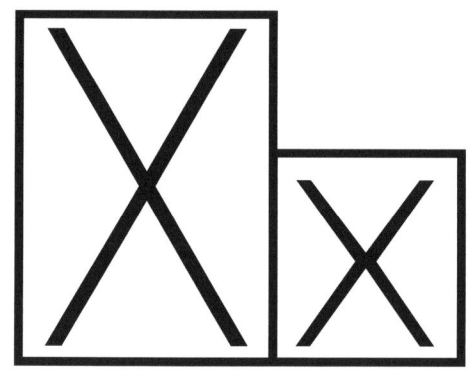

X-ray fish

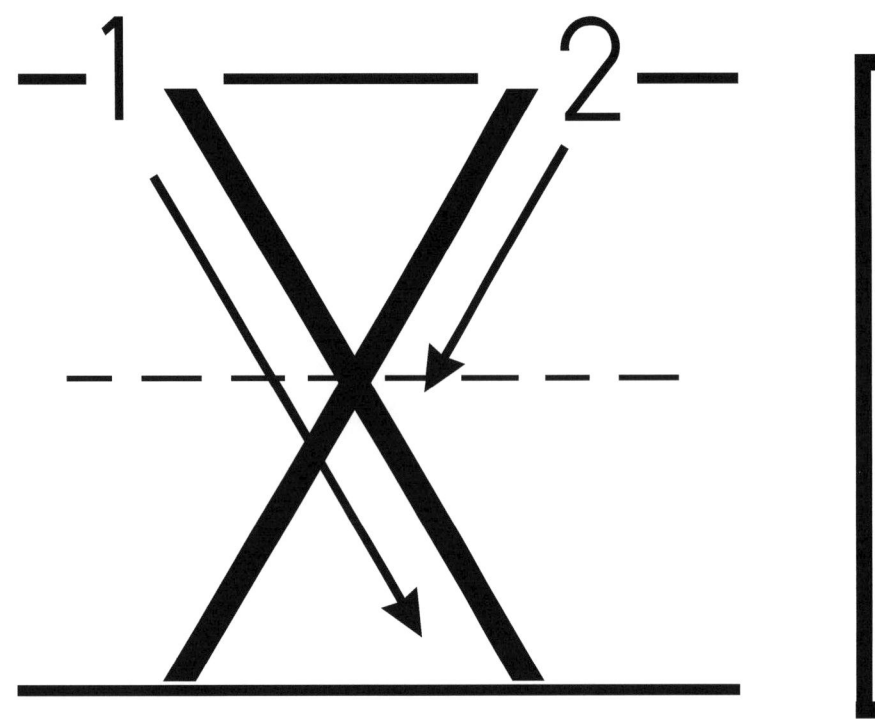

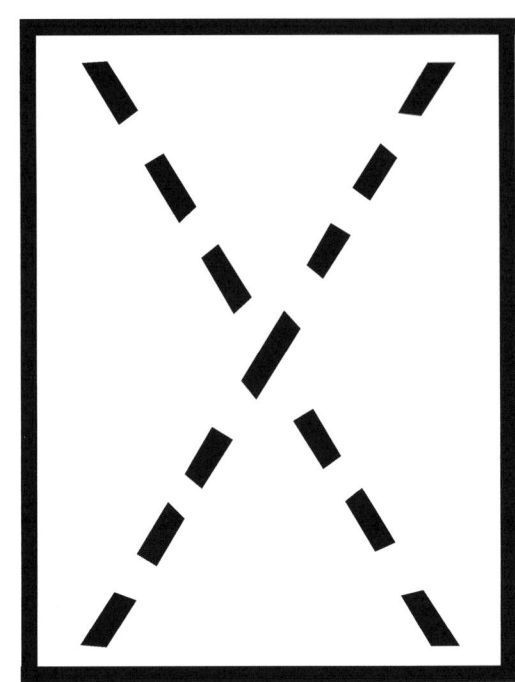

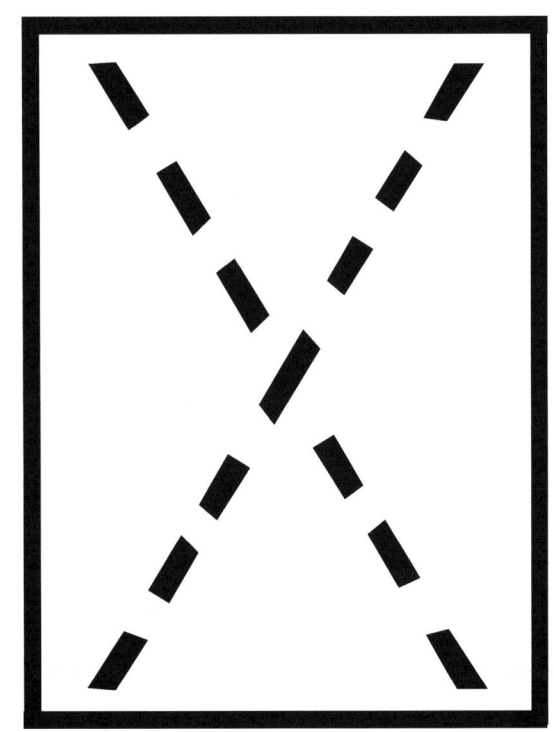

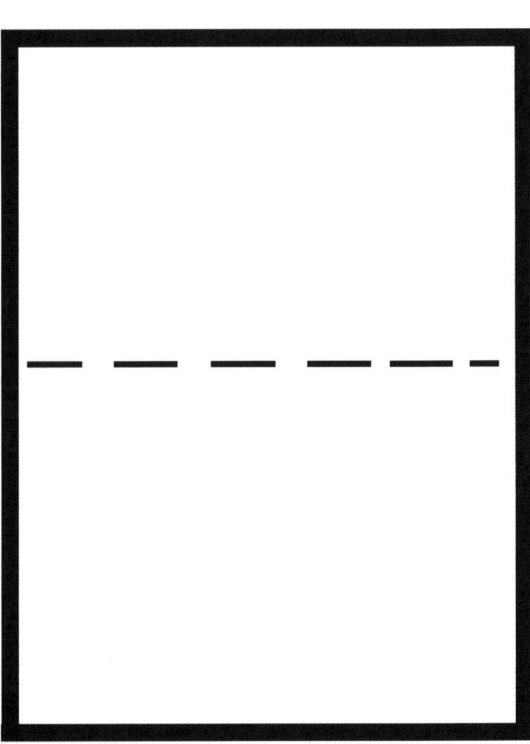

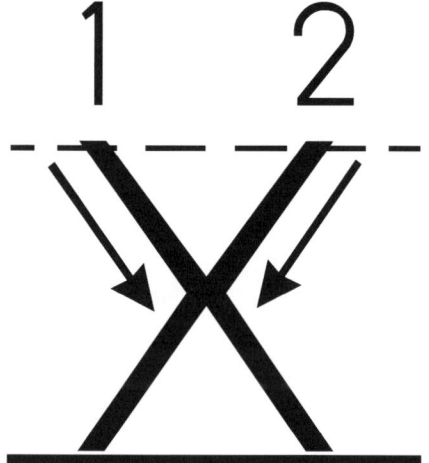

1 2

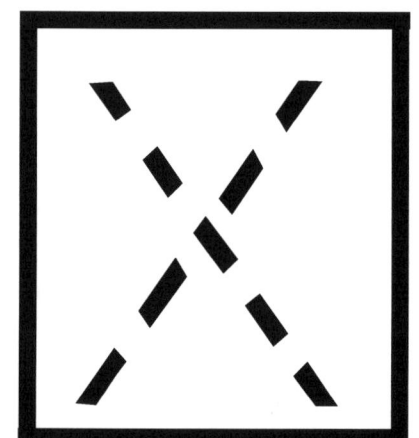

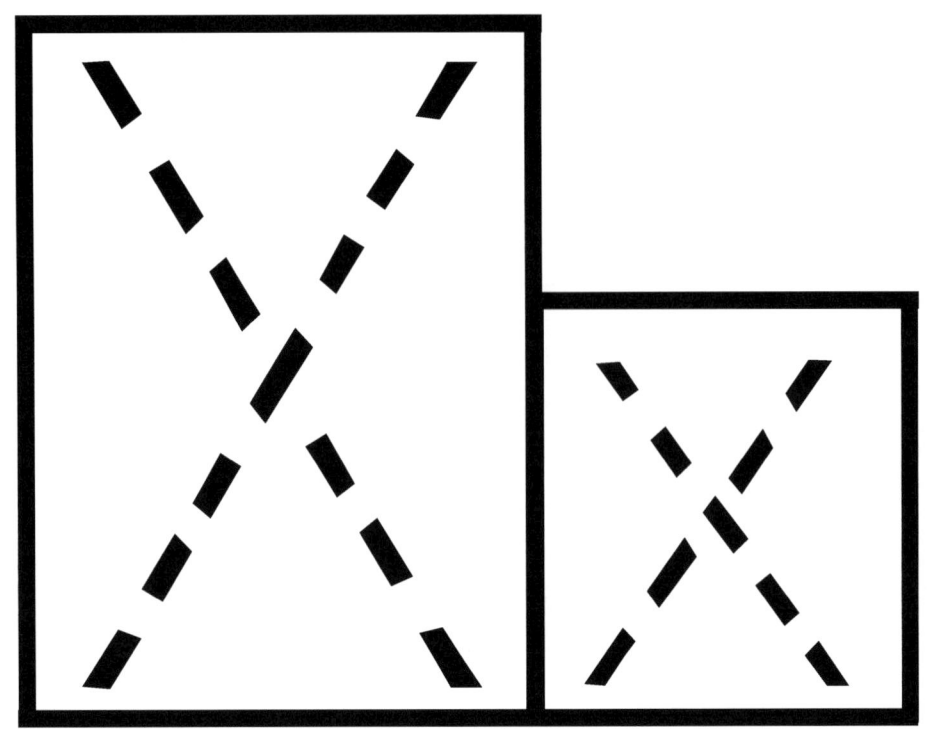

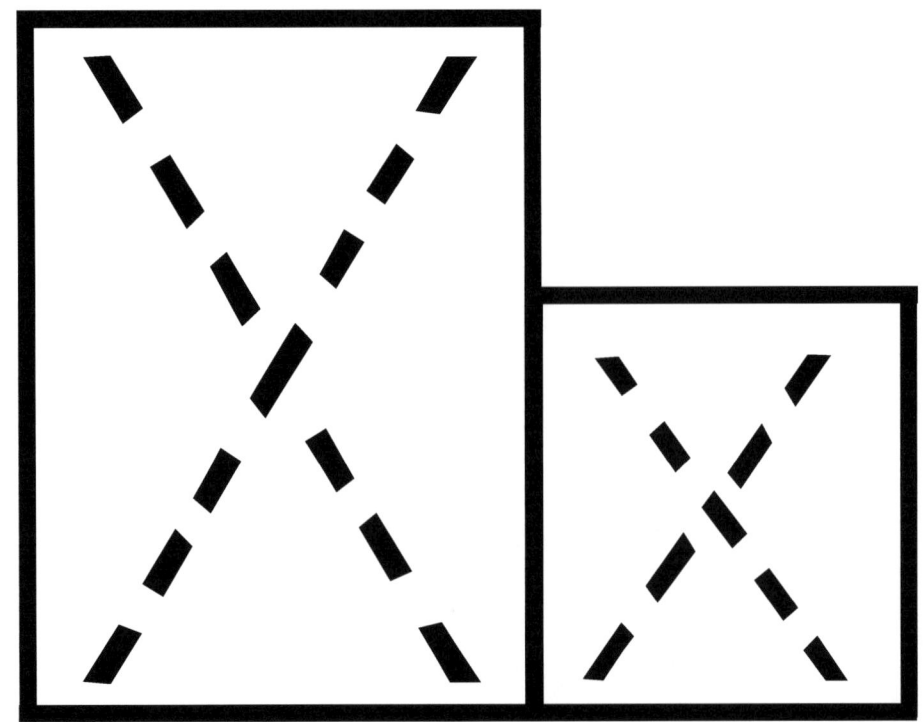

Y is for yak. Color the yak.

yak

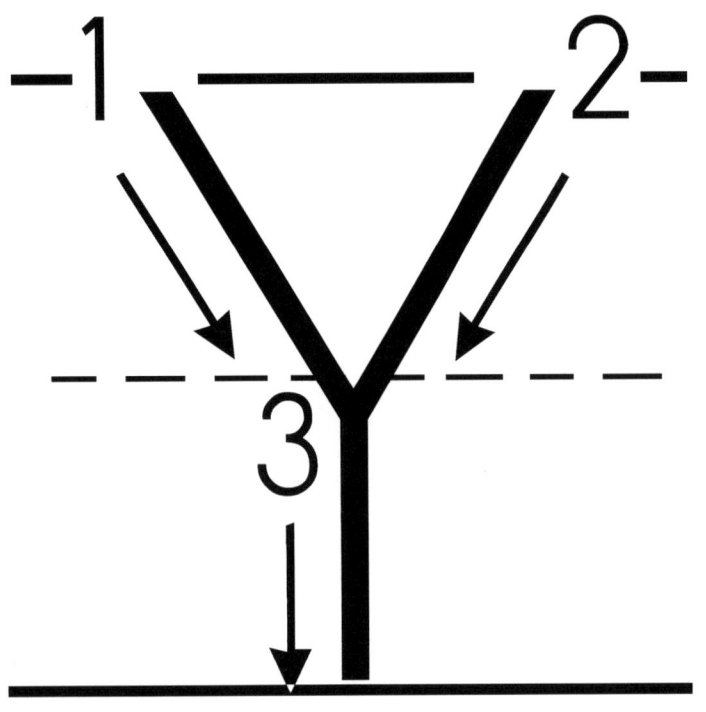
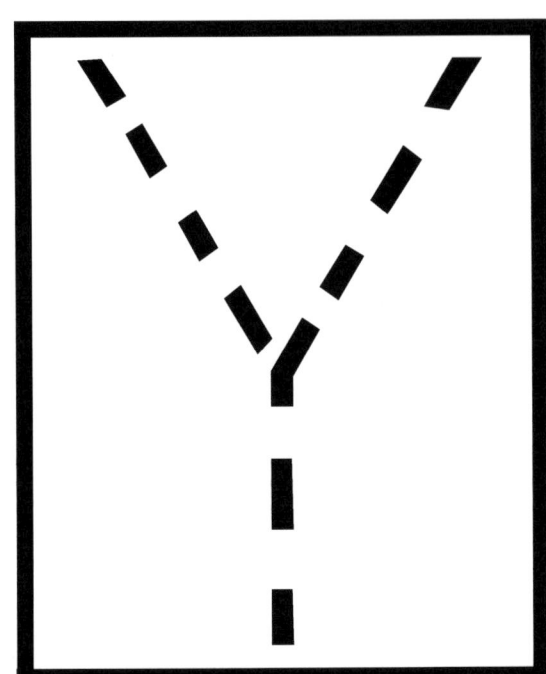
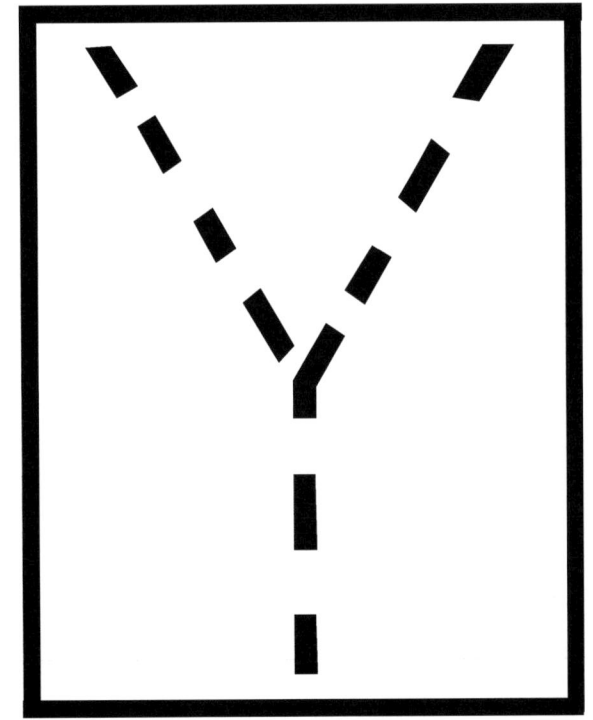
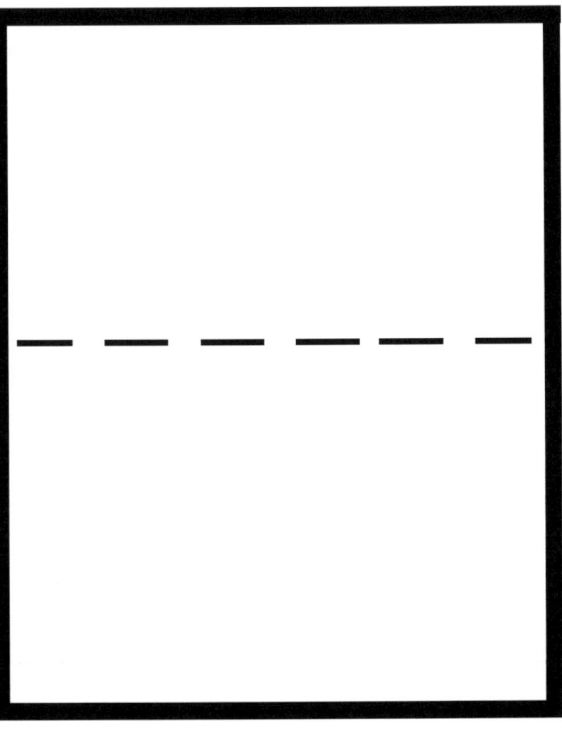

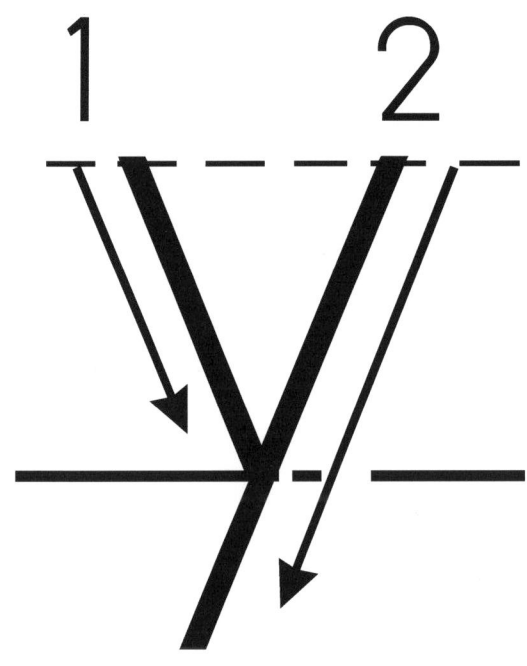

1   2

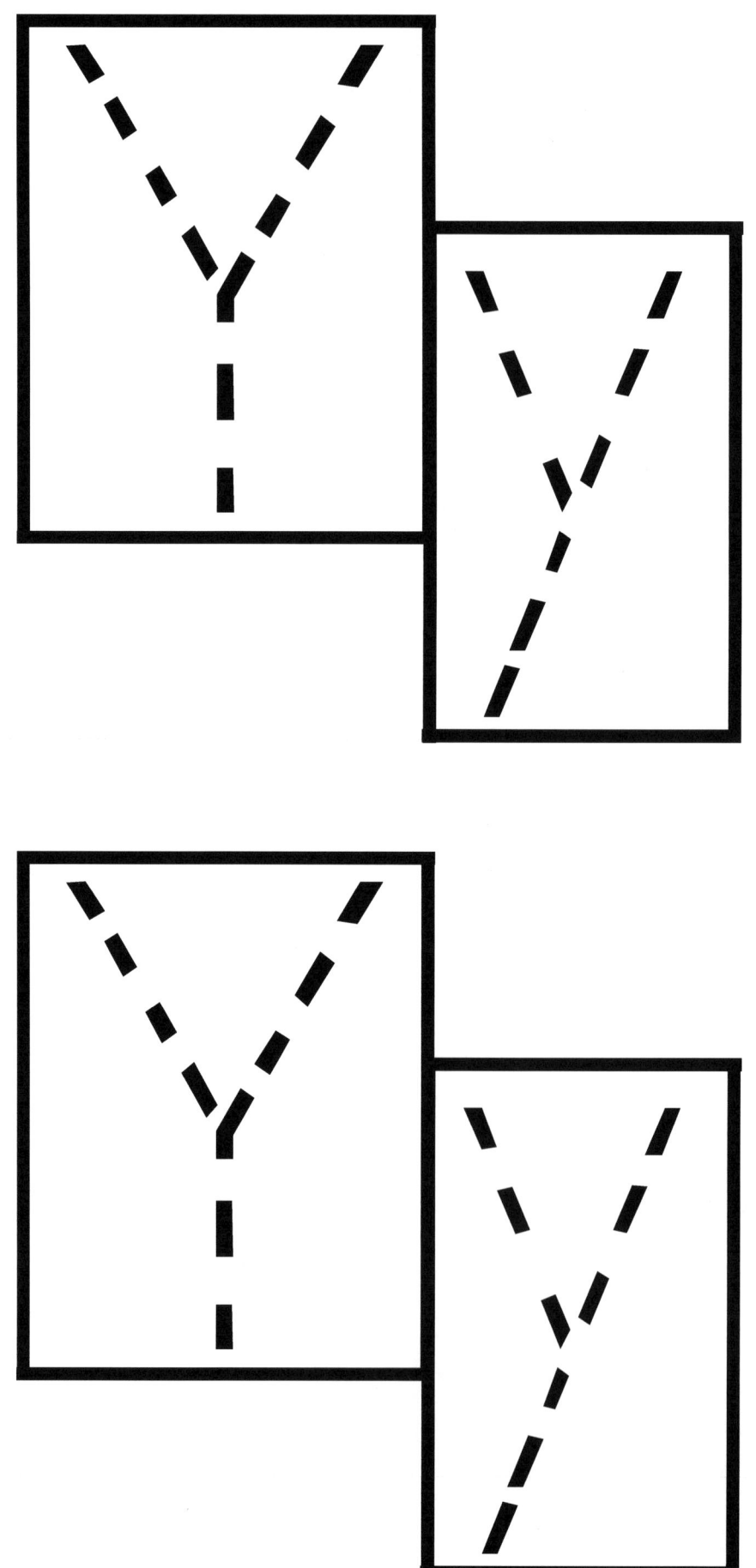

Z is for zebra. Color the zebra.

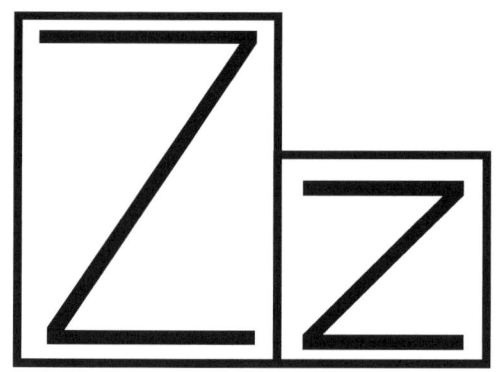

zebra

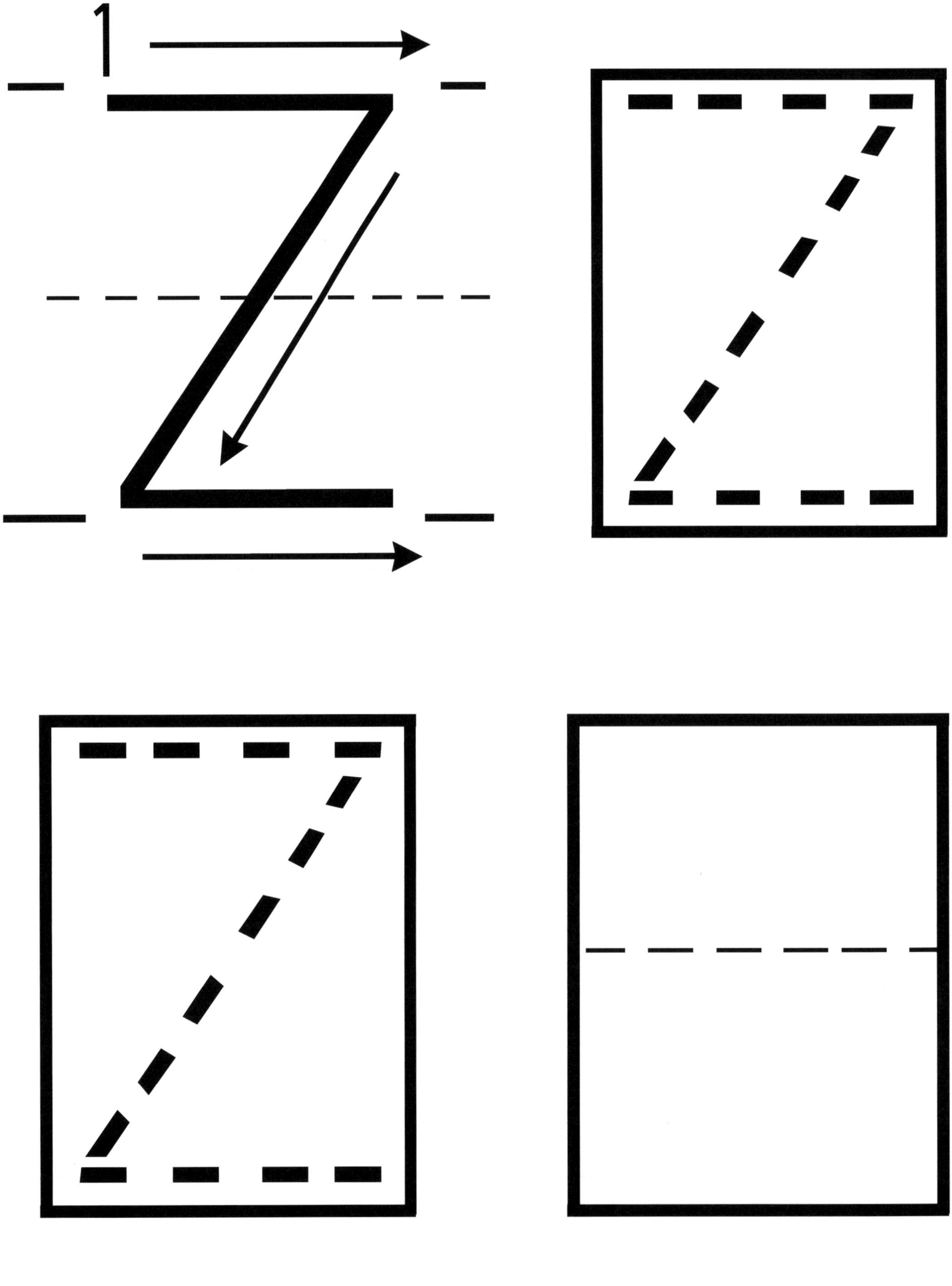

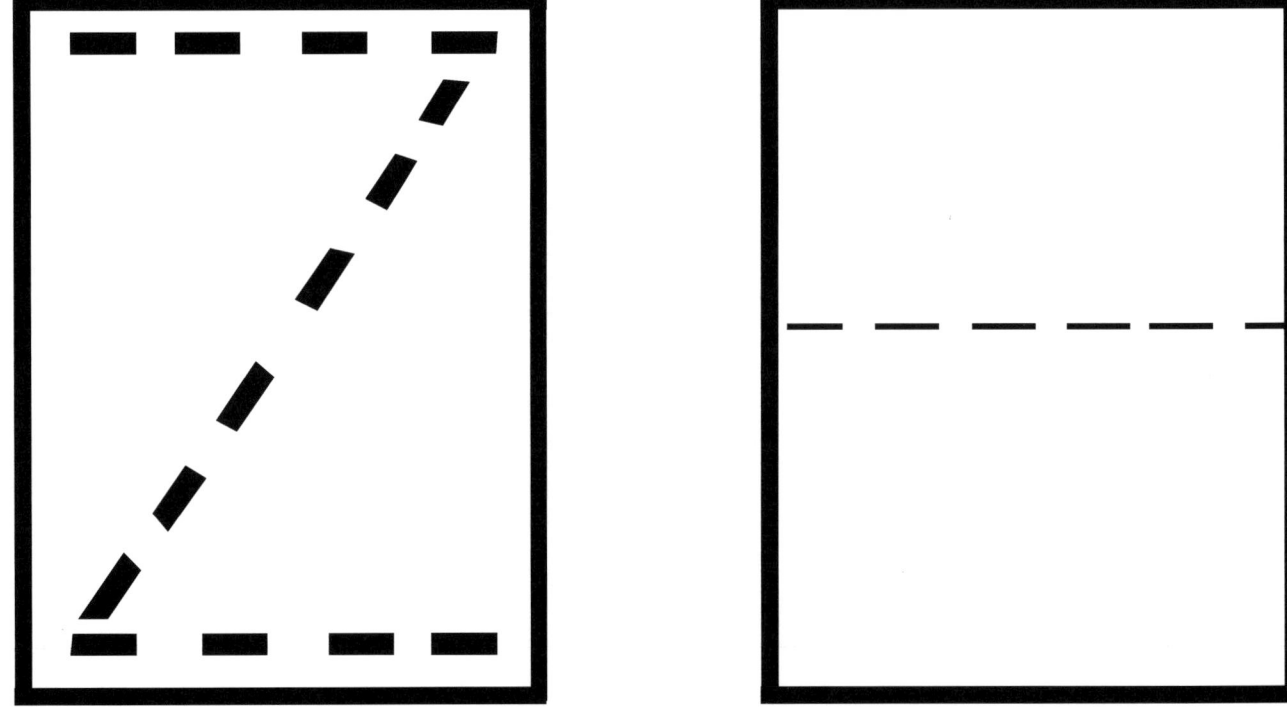

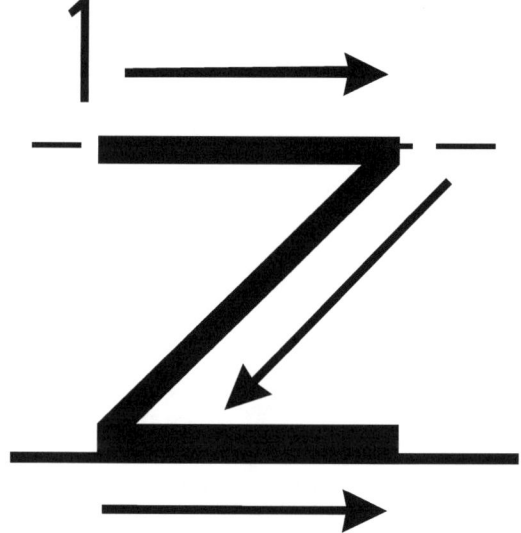

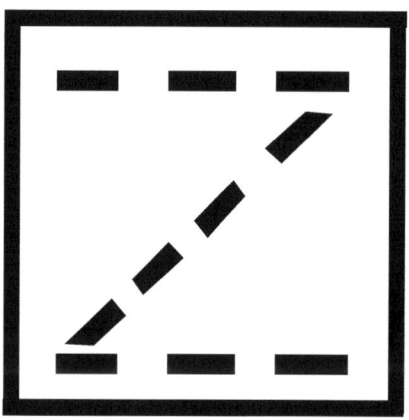

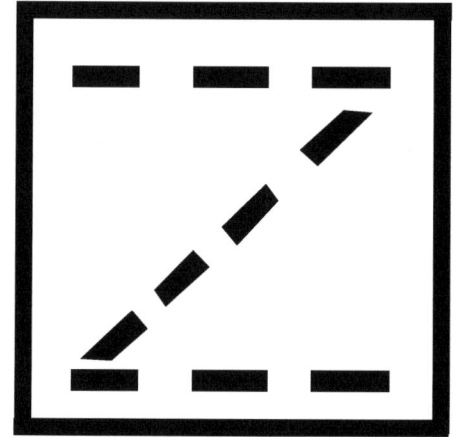

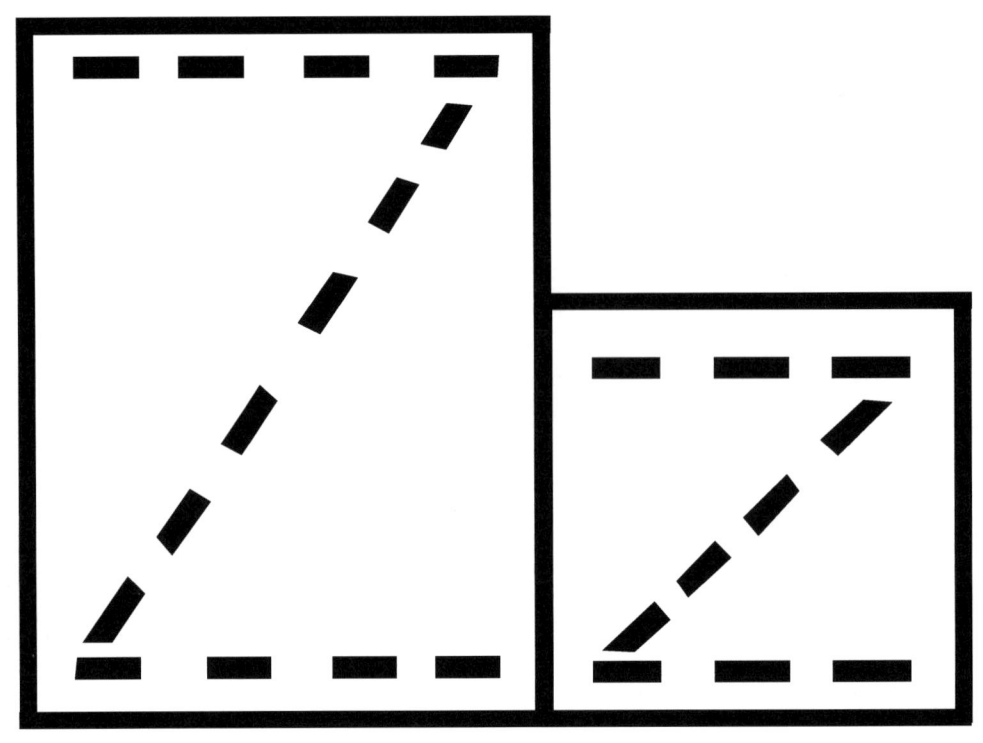

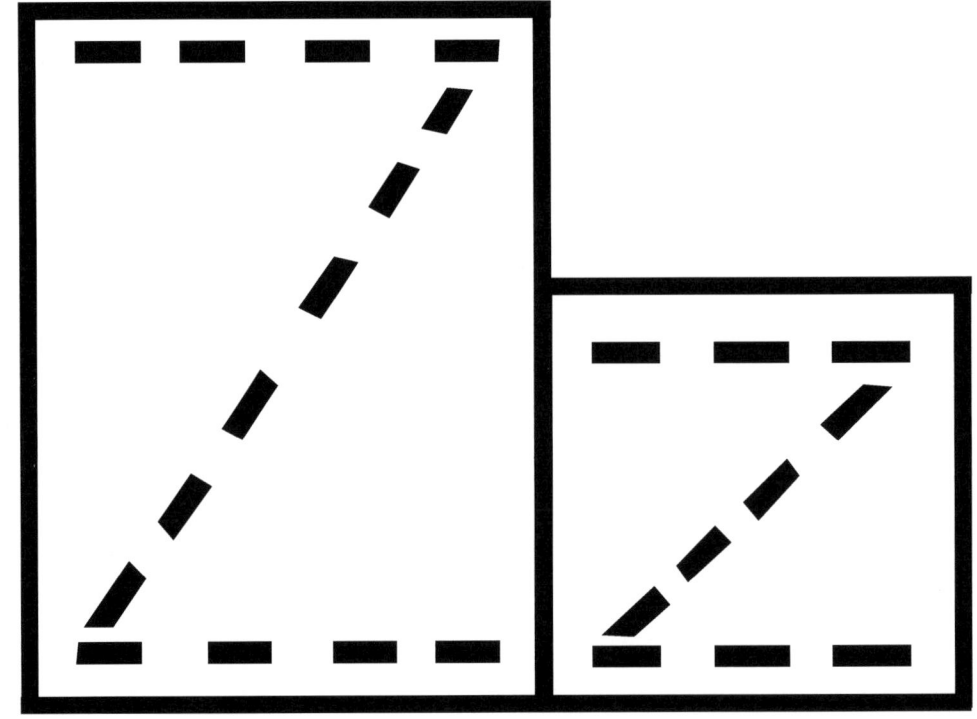

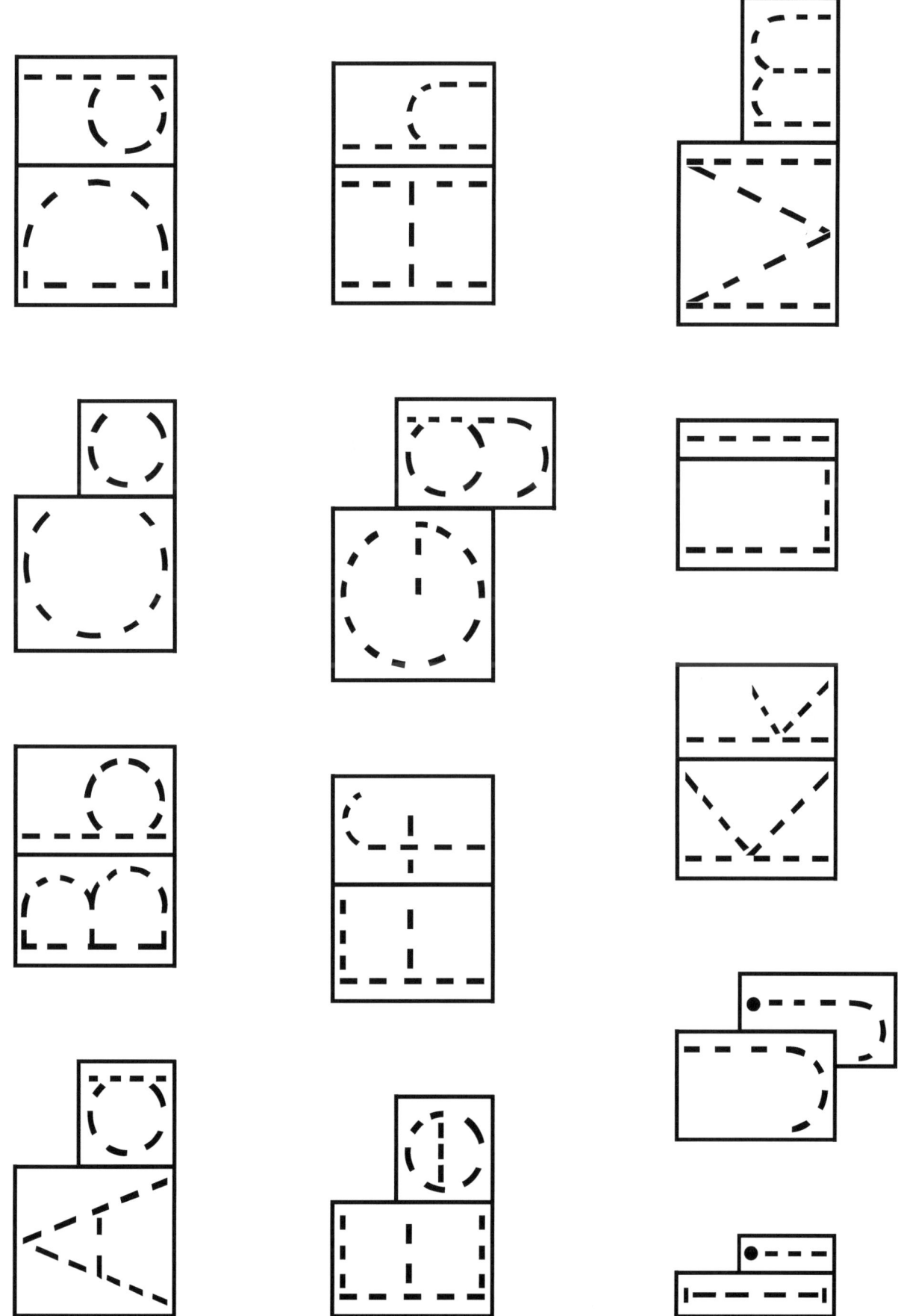

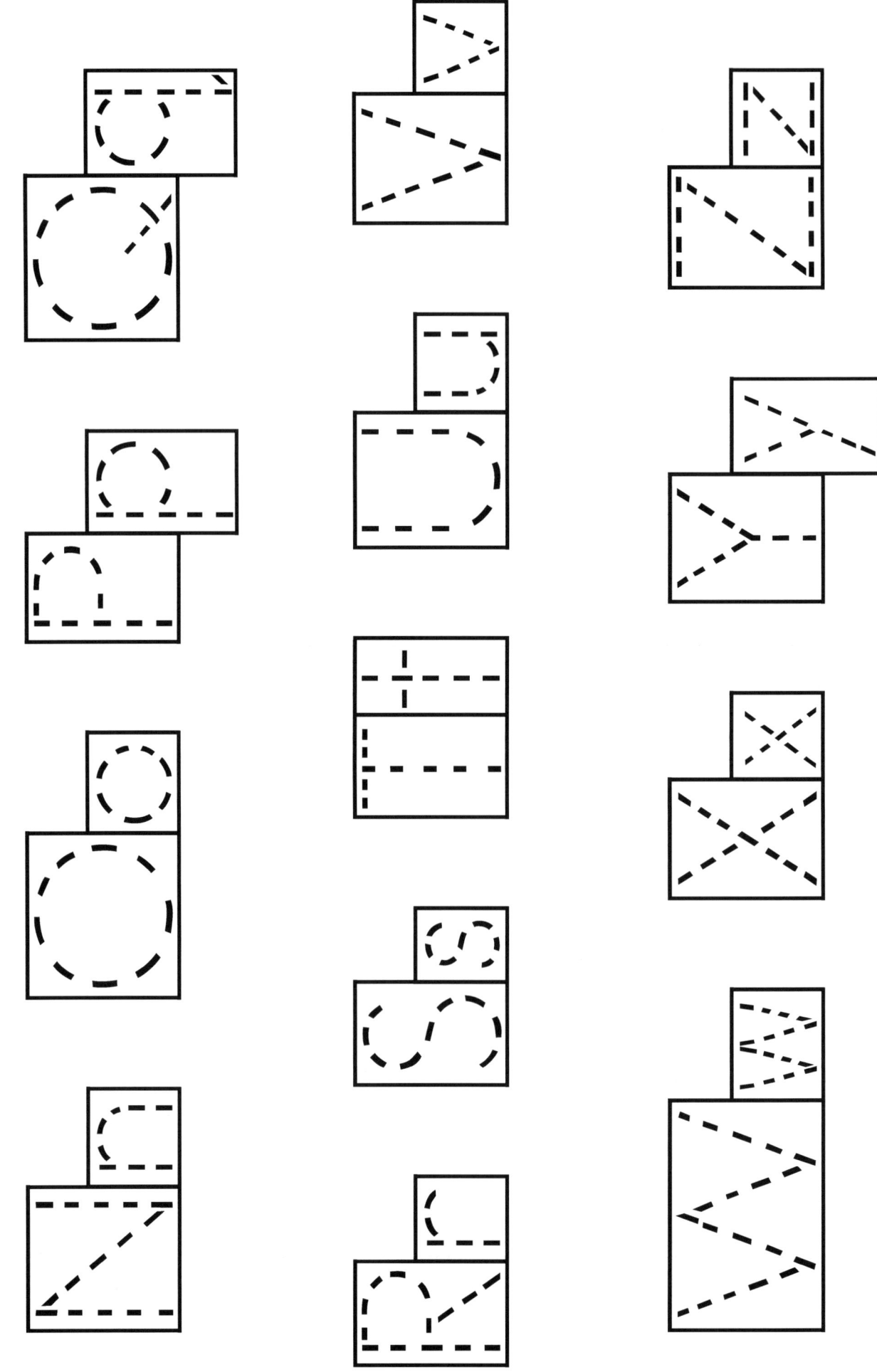

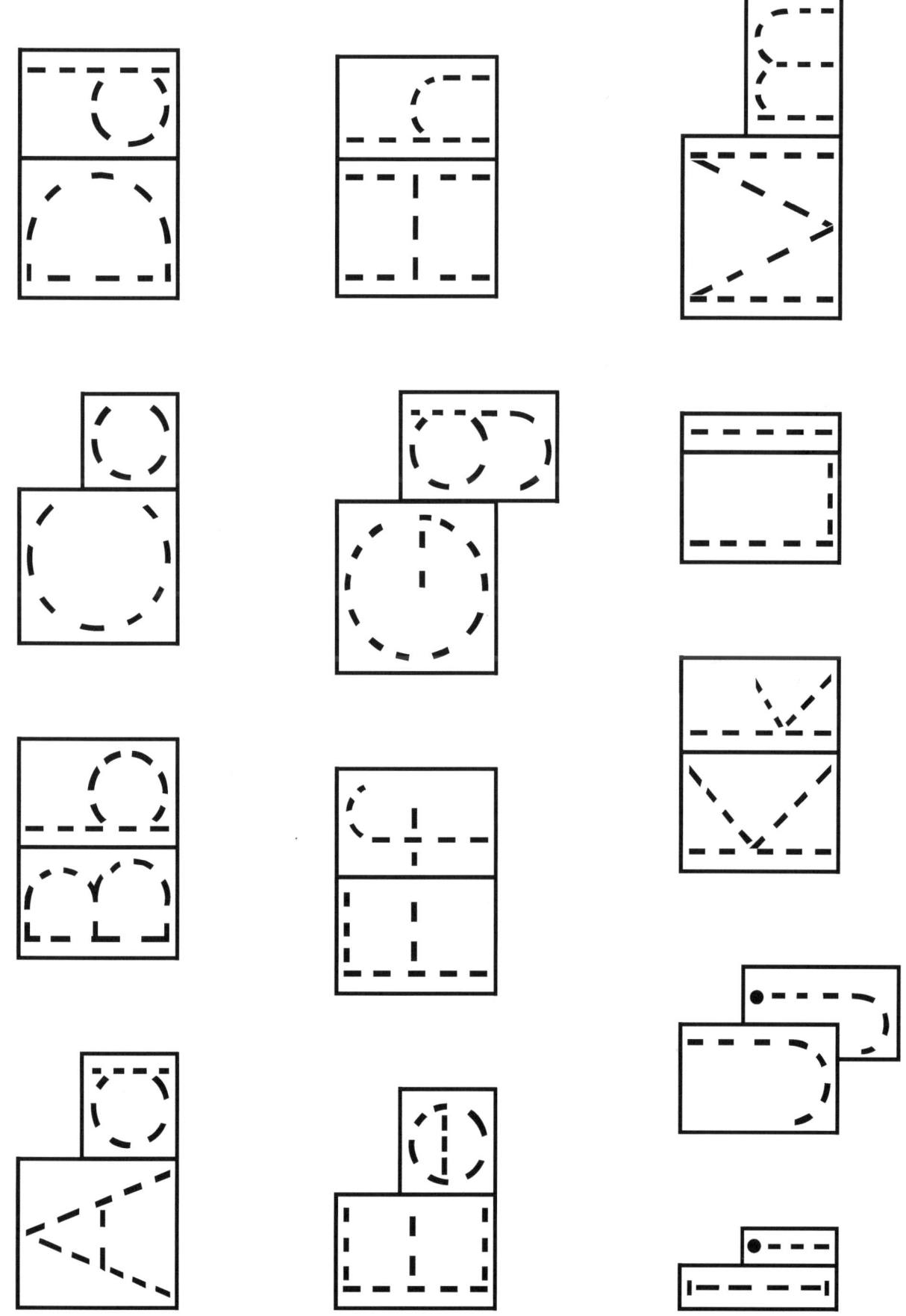

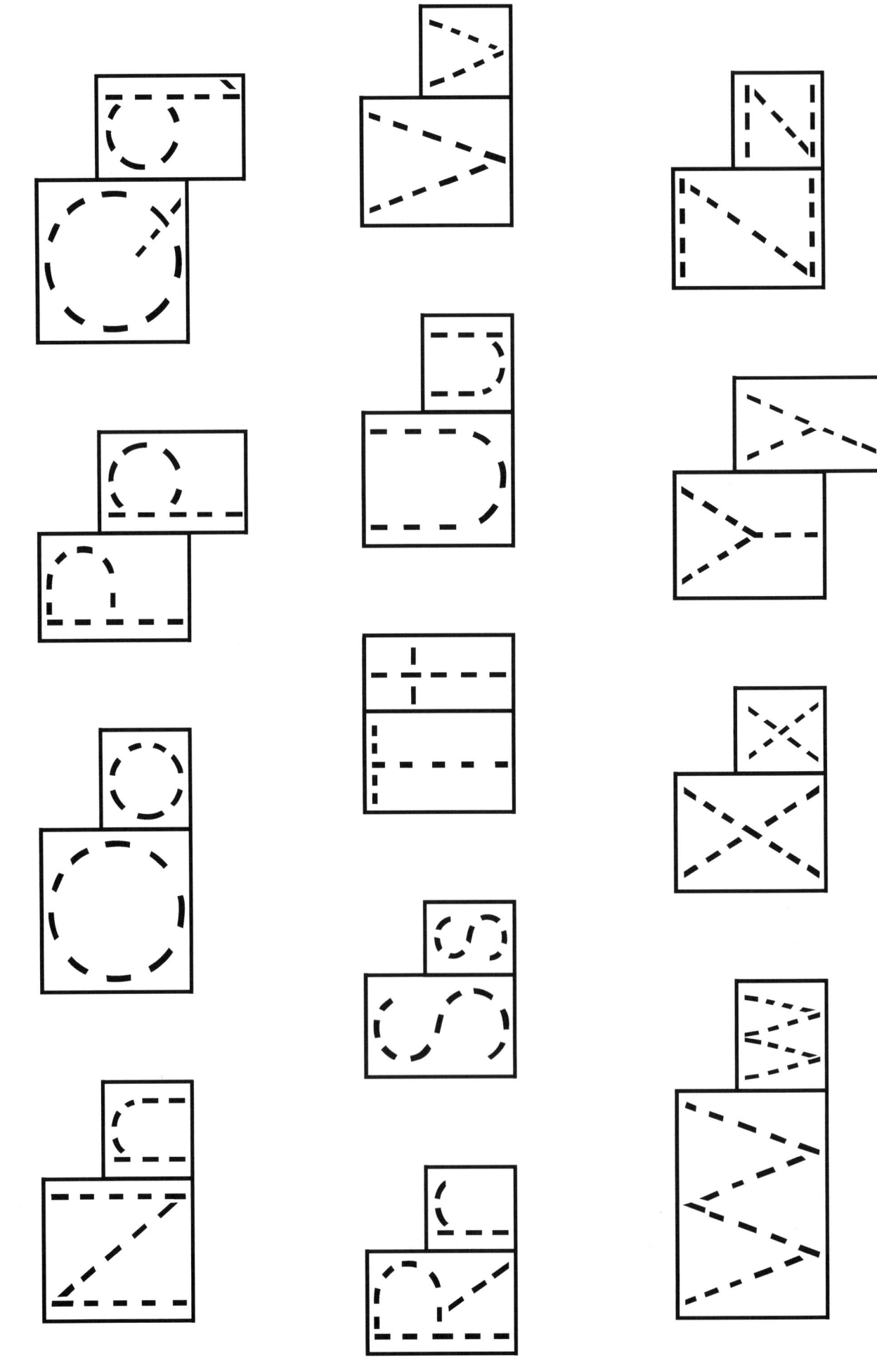

Made in United States
Troutdale, OR
03/23/2025

29978730R00064